INDIAN COOKING
Traditional Cuisine

Yes, we eat to live. But to make food palatable, we make an art of cooking, and enjoy the flavours, the odours, the colour and the texture of foods.

Many of us are adventurous in our eating habits, especially when travelling or living overseas. But though we love to experiment with foods from different countries, there's nothing like home, sweet food from home!

A large number of the recipes in this book are old favourites, recombined to achieve a change in flavour. There are also recipes which came about because some Indian ingredients were not available and substitutes had to be found. Except for a few elaborate recipes, all the dishes here are quick and easy to prepare.

Read these recipes, understand them, and get started, and you'll have for yourself a piece of heaven on a platter!

Published by
Sterling Publishers Pvt. Ltd.

Indian Cooking Overseas
Traditional Cuisine Survives

Mona Melwani

A Sterling Paperback

STERLING PAPERBACKS
An imprint of
Sterling Publishers (P) Ltd.,
L-10, Green Park Extn., New Delhi-110016

Indian Cooking Overseas
© 1995, Mona Melwani
ISBN 81 207 1613 2

All rights are reserved. No part of this publication may be reproduced, stored in a retrieval system or transmitted, in any form or by any means, mechanical, photocopying, recording or otherwise, without prior written permission of the publisher.

Published by Sterling Publishers Pvt. Ltd.
Printed at Gopsons Papers Pvt. Ltd. Noida
Cover design by Narendra Vashishta

CONTENTS

INTRODUCTION ix

TABLE OF EQUIVALENTS xiii

GLOSSARY xiv

STARTERS
- Party Fried Chicken 1
- Quick Fish Tikkas 2
- Tuna Roll-ups 3
- Chicken Chat 4
- Chicken Satay 5
- Fried Chicken Legs 6
- Spicy Chicken Wings 7
- Egg Cutlets 8
- Savoury Gram Flour Cake 9
- Lunch Box Puris 10
- Potato Scones 11

MEAT AND FISH
- Mutton Vindaloo 12
- Mutton Chops with Yoghurt 13
- Ground Mutton Pie 14
- Mutton Curry 16
- Rich Mutton Mutanjan 17
- Mutton Pasanda 19
- Chicken Royale 20
- Chicken Chilli 21
- Chicken Palak 22

Rich Indian Chicken Curry	23
Chicken Curry with Cummin	24
Cheesy Chicken Submarine	25
Black Pepper Chicken	26
Egg Vindaloo	27
Hyderabad Chicken	28
Chinese Prawn Balls	29
Party Prawn Curry	30
Fried Prawn Rice	32
Pork Ribs in Sweet and Sour Sauce	34
Sri Lankan Fish Curry	35
Singapore Noodles	36
Baked Macaroni and Ham	37

VEGETARIAN DELIGHTS

Malai Kofta with an Italian Touch	38
Paneer Cashewnut Curry	40
Cauliflower Spinach Sukha	41
Mushrooms Au Gratin	42
Instant Lasagna	43
Party Vegetarian Lasagna	44
Fettuchini Alfredo	46
Brinjal Curry	48
Greek Macaroni Salad	49
Fruity Cabbage Salad	50
Sauteed Mushrooms	51
Quick Cook Dal-Cha	52
Cabbage Cutlets	53
Green Peas and Cashewnut Curry	54
Seyal Cheese Macaroni Bake	56
Goanese Potatoes	57
Sukha Okra	58
Sukha Eggplant	59
Capsicum Pulao	60
Potatoes in Green Gravy	61
Indonesian Curry	62
Ginger Flavoured Cauliflower	63
Cauliflower Spinach Sukha	64
Mushroom with Yoghurt	65
Cabbage Manchurian	66
Macaroni Mushroom Bake	68

Potato and Eggplant Curry	69
Cheese Kofta Curry	70
Peas Mushroom Curry	72
Baked Mixed Vegetable Pie	73
Spicy Mixed Vegetable Pie	74
Spinach Mushroom Bake	76

CAKES AND DESSERTS

Russian Tea Cakes	77
Carrot Cake	78
Nutritious Oatmeal Biscuits	79
Basic Muffins	80
Cornflake Macaroons	82
Turkish Delight	83
Indian Butter Cookies	84
Irish Tea Bread	85
No-Bake Cheesecake (Vegetarian)	86
Fruit and Nut Bars	88
Crazy Cake (Vegetarian)	89
Rich Trifle Pudding (Vegetarian)	90
Easy Chocolate Cake	92
Quick Crisp Dessert	93
Apple Upside-Down Cake	94
Fresh Apple Cake	95
Candy Bar Pie	96
Pineapple and Jelly Delight	97
Baked Semolina Pudding	98
Apple Ginger Tarts	99
Creamy Lemon Pie	100
Gingered Pears	101
Creamy Marshmallow Dessert	102
Fruit and Nut Dessert	103
English Trifle	104
Mango Mousse	105
Cherry Delight	106
Apple Torte	107
Short Crust Dough	108

ALPHABETIC LIST OF RECIPES　　　　　　　109

AN APPETIZER.... I MEAN AN INTRODUCTION

Food is fascinating. Its variety is matched only by the combined creativity of the communities of the world. Today as we get more global and more informed about nutrition and health, and as new products are being declared edible, this creativity is challenged because food continues to be a basic human need.

Food is a science, only so far as the chemistry of food affects the chemistry of the human body. Everything else about it, I feel, is art. Long ago, I used to think that the art was in the fine ideas that have made vegetable carving and cake decoration so popular. Anyone who has watched the vegetable carver at the Taipei Hilton turn a carrot into a big fishing net and registered the "Ah!" that escapes when the carrot chiselling is completed and in one dramatic motion the net is flung open, will swear that this is indeed art.

More intrinsic however, is the novel ways we combine food to make heaven on a platter! I originally sub-titled this book *Traditional Cuisine Survives*, because in Taiwan I found myself cooking with ingredients which either did not figure in my culinary dictionary or I didn't use as often before. Mushrooms, apples, spring onions, fresh garlic stems, canned soup for gravy base, are a few examples. Yet these ingredients are not strange or unknown, just indigenous to Taiwan. I found myself playing with ideas to use them in ways that would appeal to my particular Indian palate. Then I met other Indian women in Taiwan doing the same thing and so was born this book.

Many of the recipes here are old favourites - recombined to achieve a change in flavour. Redoing age-old combinations can bring some exciting results.

The plentiful supply of resonably priced products available here, encouraged the creation of some of the 'Recipes with a difference'. Things like evaporated milk, fruit cocktail, sour cream, cream cheese, graham crackers.

Then there are recipes which came about because some Indian ingredients were not available here and substitutes had to be found. When you come to a place where there are no dals, and wheat flour, and fine grained rice, panic bells begin to ring. How does one live without these our daily staples. In blind panic you say 'there's nothing available here'! You do not see the yellow mung dal, rajma, green mung, chole, in neat clear plastic bags stacked on market shelves. You are surprised that coriander leaves are easy to recognise and sign with relief that you have a substitute for mint (pudina). What a life-saver, chutney will now be possible, if only tamarind (imli) was more accessible than a trip to Hong Kong.

The Taiwan customs are now accustomed to the fragrances of our masalas, the bags of atta and rice and dals our luggage is full of when we return from Hong Kong. For those of us who, when in India, made dream lists of imported cosmetics and perfumes to get from Hong Kong, there is a sweet vengeance in shopping instead for dal and atta.

Culinary culture appears to fuflil an instinctual need. Why else do we choose to even hand carry the extra kilo of besan instead of that second handbag? Why does dal bath sound heavenly in the midst of fast food chains and delicatessans? For this reason I have included a few old favourites. Often these veterans are changed so much that one forgets what the original was like. I feel that the originals must on continue to be learned as a foundation to build new ideas; we keep our culture and traditions alive as much by practicing our recipes as we do by our dances and our music. Food is a cultural memory we must continuously transfer to our children. Let me show you what I mean.

Think of a comfort food, something you desire to eat when

you are happy, or sad or sick... or in need of comfort. Recall the time when you used to eat it. The chances are that the food you thought of was something your Mother made for you when you were sick, or your Father bought for you. Chances equally are that it was a family celebration favourite. You will find that the food was eaten at occasions the memory of which is dear to you. This is cultural memory — the basis on which tradition survives.

Except for a few elaborate recipes, all the dishes here are easy and quick, as I have kept in mind the working woman. Most recipes list ingredients which are usually available in every Indian kitchen. Really, there are very few things you should try to substitute.

The recipes in this book have been tried and tested in many kitchens and are imminently workable - if you make them as you are supposed to . More likely, here are two things you might do.

Read the recipe, understand it and get started. As you go on, you decide to add an ingredient sooner than you are supposed to or in other ways change the order. You do this because of your years of experience in the kitchen, or simply because your hands are wet or greasy and you can't turn the page. "It all goes in there anyway," you say. To really appreciate the author's intention I feel the directions should be followed exactly as stated, at least the first time. This is the only way to know the flavour, colour and texture that was intended. Changes can be made, to suit your preference, the next time round.

Another thing you may do is sustitute one ingredient for another, but the substitute you use may not yield the desired flavour. Think of sustituting anise (saunf) seed for cummin seed (zeera) and you will understand what I mean. On the other hand if you hit on a combination that really worked, I would love to hear it.

A quick glance through these pages will reveal that there is no fair distribution of salads, desserts, main dishes and the like. My intention has not been to give you a book with that sort of balance. I wish to share with you my favourite recipes, those that are easy, tasty and fail-proof.

Finally, acknowledgements are in order to the Eve's Group of Taipei, whose members demonstrated and shared their cooking adventures with me. My thanks to all of them.

Special thanks to my husband, Murli, my son, Arvind, and my daughter, Arpan. Their patience, constructive criticism and willingness to analyse flavours of a meal long after it was digested has been invaluable.

Mona Melwani
Taipei, Taiwan

Table of Equivalents

3 teaspoons = 1 tablespoon
4 tablespoons = $1/4$ cup liquid
1 cup = 8 ounces = $1/2$ pint
2 cups = 1 pint
4 cups = 1 quart
4 quart = 1 gallon
1 litre = 1.06 quarts
28.35 grams = 1 ounce
100 grams = $3^1/2$ ounces
1 kilo = 1000 grams = 2 pounds, 3 ounces
454 grams = 1 pound = 16 ounces

Butter

1 ounce = 2 tablespoons = $1/8$ cup
2 ounces = 4 tablespoons = $1/4$ cup
4 ounces = 8 tablespoons = $1/2$ cup = 1 stick = $1/4$ pound

Oven Temperatures

	Degrees Fahrenheit	Degree Centigrade
Very slow	250	121
Slow	325	163
Moderate	350	177
Hot	450	232

Garam Masala

10 gms each of cardamom, shahjeera, cinnamon, cloves, black pepper, 2-3 bay leaves. Heat in a skillet and grind into a fine powder. Store in an airtight jar.

Glossary

English	Hindi equivalents
Asafoetida	Hing
Aniseed	Sonf
Basil	Tulsi (dried)
Black Salt	Kala Namak
Caraway Seed	Shahi Jeera
Cardamon	Elaichi
Clarified butter	Ghee
Cloves	Lavang
Coriander	Dhania
Cummin seed	Jeera
Dry Coconut	Copra
Dry Mango Powder	Amchoor
Fenugreek Seeds	Methi or Methre
Garlic	Lehsan
Ginger	Adrak
Gingelly Seeds	Til
Garden Cress Seeds	Halim
Gramflour	Besan
Lemon Leaves	Neem Ka Patta
Mint	Pudina
Mace	Javithri
Mustard Seeds	Sarson or Rai
Nutmeg	Jaiphal
Onion Seeds	Pyaz ka Beej
Peppercorns	Kali Mirch
Poppy Seeds	Khus-khus
Red Chillies (Dry)	Sukhi Lal Mirch
Salt Petx	Shora
Saffron	Zafran or Kesar
Spinach	Palak
Star Aniseed	Badyan
Tamarind	Imli
Turmeric	Haldi
Thymol Seeds	Ajwain
Wheat Flour	Atta

Party Snacks and Starters

Party Fried Chicken

INGREDIENTS

Marinade
1 dozen chicken
  legs (small)
4 tbsp soya sauce
4 tbsp lemon juice
1 tsp salt

Batter
1/2 cup water
2 tbsp oil
2 egg whites
1 tbsp baking powder
1/2 tsp salt
3/4 cup flour
1/2 tsp ajinomoto
1/4 cup ground cashewnuts
  (optional)
oil for deep frying

METHOD

Marinate chicken legs in the marinade mixture for about two hours. Combine the batter ingredients and mix well. Coat the chicken in the batter and deep fry till golden brown. Chicken should be crisp outside and tender within. It is loved by children and adults alike.

Quick Fish Tikkas

INGREDIENTS

1 can tuna fish
1 small potato
1 slice of bread
2 green chillies
1/2 tsp each : coriander, salt,
    garam masala, black pepper
    and cummin powder

1 tbsp lemon juice
few sprigs of coriander leaves
oil for deep frying

METHOD

Drain all the water or oil from tuna can. Remove tuna and flake. Boil and mash potato. Soak bread in water, then squeeze it all out. Mix together the fish, potato and bread. Add all the other spices, the coriander leaves and lemon juice and mix well. Grease a drop of oil on your hands to shape this mixture into tikkas. Tikkas can be fried directly or covered with breadcrumbs. Tasty eaten hot with a hot sauce.

Tuna Roll-ups

INGREDIENTS

1 cup sharp cheddar cheese
1 can tuna drained and flaked
1 tbsp lemon juice
1 green chilli finely chopped
2 tsps lemon juice

3/4 tsp salt to taste
1/4 tsp black pepper
1/2 whipped cream cheese
20 slices soft white bread
1/2 cups pound melted butter
chopped coriander leaves
1 lemon

METHOD

Preheat the over to 300° F. Mix together cheese, tuna fish, onion, green chilli, lemon juice, salt and pepper. Soften the cream cheese and whip it up to make a smooth spreadable mixture. Add this cream cheese to the tuna-cheese mixture and blend well with a fork. Now add the coriander leaves. Cut the corners of each slice of bread and gently roll over it with a rolling pin. Spread the tuna mixture evenly and roll each slice. Wet the edges with water or egg white and seal. Brush melted butter on each tunaroll-up and bake at 300 degrees F. for 15 minutes. Tastes good event without ketchup. Great with drinks.

Chicken Chaat

INGREDIENTS

2 breasts boneless chicken
1 cup yoghurt
1 tsp each of the following :
    chilli powder, garam masala, cummin powder, coriander powder, chaat masala, rock salt (kala namak)
    hing.

1/2 tsp tandoori colour
5-6 tbsps clove powder
1 tsp tamarind
10 cloves garlic
4 green chillies
2 inch piece ginger.
1 large onion
3 tbsp oil

METHOD

If you are using a blender : put the ginger, garlic, green chillies and lemon juice and grind together. Then put in the following powders: coriander, clove, garam masala, rock salt to taste, and chill. Blend till smooth.

  Wash and clean chicken and cut into bite size cubes. Marinate with the blended mixture for five to six hours. Meanwhile cut half the onion in long slices and chop the other half finely. Using a frying pan, heat the oil, put in the cummin seeds and the asafoetida a few seconds later. Fry till slightly browned and then add the chopped onion. Stir and add the chicken. Mix and allow to cook uncovered till the chicken is tender. When the spices are all absorbed, pour into bake-proof serving dish and bake for ten minutes. Sprinkle chaat masala, slivers of green chillies and fried sliced onion. Serve hot.

Chicken Satay

INGREDIENTS

2 chicken breasts
1/2 cup soya sauce
salt to taste
2 bell peppers
2 carrots
2 onions
2 cups of pineapple chunks

Method

Remove skin. Clean and wash the chicken. Cut into 1/2 to 3/4 inch pieces. Mix the salt with the soya souce and put the chicken pieces in it to marinate for about an hour. Cut carrot and peppers to match size of chicken pieces.

Use wooden skewers, which are available. If not, use metal skewers. Insert or thread a piece of chicken on a skewer, then put in a cube of carrot, a piece of bell pepper and then a chunk of pineapple. This sequence can be followed twice or thrice on a single skewer. The last five inches of the skewer must be kept free for holding and to facilitate cooking.

Pour a tablespoon of oil on a griddle or tava and arrange the satays on it. Cook on medium-high heat. The vegetables should remain somewhat crunchy. The chicken pieces do not take long to cook because the pieces are small and the marinade has helped to tenderize them. Satays can be cooked on a grill or open barbecue. Must be eaten sizzling hot.

Fried Chicken Legs

INGREDIENTS

8 chicken legs
(4 legs including thighs)
1 tsp turmeric
4 red chillies
1 1/2 tsp each of minced
    ginger, coriander
    powder, black pepper

1 tsps garam masala
4 cloves garlic
juice of 1 lemon
1 cup flour
1 egg
salt to taste
oil for deep frying

METHOD

If you are using the chicken leg with thigh, cut into two pieces. Rub the pieces with turmeric, ginger and salt and set aside. Grind together the garlic and red chillies. Add to this all the other ingredients except the oil for frying and the chicken. Add a few tablespoons of water and blend the mixture to make a thick coatable batter. Dip each piece of chicken in this batter. Allow to coat all sides. Then fry in hot oil till brown. This batter can be used for fish as well. For vegetarians subsitude eggplant and cauliflower for chicken. The batter needs to be less thick for vegetables.

Spicy Chicken Wings

INGREDIENTS

1 dozen chicken wings (only the upper wing portion, not the flabby lower wing portion)
1 cup yoghurt
1/2 onion chopped
5 cloves garlic
1 tsp ginger, ground
1 tsp red chilli powder
1 tsp black pepper powder
1/2 tsp cummin powder
1/2 tsp garam masala
1 tsp tomato ketchup

METHOD

Excluding the last two ingredients, put all the ingredients together and marinate the chicken with it. Keep away in fridge for about an hour. Put two teaspoons of oil. In a deep frying pan or wok, and when heat it. Put in the grated onion. Fry the onion till it becomes pink. Put in the chicken with all of the marinade, stir briskly and cook uncovered. When the chicken is tender, reduce fire and add the ketchup. Serve hot with a sprinkling of garam masala.

Egg Cutlets

INGREDIENTS

60 gms plain flour	2 eggs for coating
200 ml milk	2 green chillies
40 gms cheese	50 gms margarine
small bunch of coriander leaves	4 hardboiled eggs, shelled and chopped
salt and pepper to taste	breadcrumbs

METHODS

Heat the margarine and when melted add the flour slowly, cooking it without browning it (takes about a minute or less). Add milk and mix to help smooth the mixture. When the white sauce is thick, put the fire off and then add all the ingredients except the eggs and the breadcrumbs. These will be used later for coating the cutlets. The mixture should be firm. Divide into sixteen balls and then shape them into cutlets. Dip each cutlet in the beaten eggs and then roll in breadcrumbs. Deep fry till light brown and crisp.

Savory Gram Flour Cake

INGREDIENTS

1 1/2 cups gram flour (besan)
1/2 cup oil
1 tsp bicarbonate of soda
2 tbsps finely chopped onion
1 cup yoghurt
2 eggs
1 tbsp ground red chillies (or to taste)
4 green chillies
salt to taste

METHOD

Put together the besan, oil, soda, yoghurt, eggs and salt. Mix well with a beater or in the blender. Now fold in the coriander leaves, chopped onion, green and red chillies. Pour the mixture in a baking tin and bake at 300 degrees F for about 40 minutes or until cake is browned on top and a toothpick inserted comes out clean. Good tea time snack. May be eaten hot or cold.

Lunch Box Puris

INGREDIENTS

2 cups wheat flour
1 cup plain white flour
2 tsps baking powder
2 tsps ghee or butter or oil
1 cup yoghurt

2 tsps cummin
1 tsp chilli powder
1 tsp ground black pepper
salt to taste (about 1 level tsp)
oil for frying

METHOD

Mix well the first list of ingredients. Then add the second list of ingredients. Knead dough well, till firm but elastic. Cover and keep for an hour. Roll out into puris and deep fry. These spicy puris taste good even when they are cold and make a good lunch-box, picnic or train travel companion.

Potato Scones

INGREDIENTS

3/4 ounces self-raising flour 6 tbsps butter
1/2 level tsp ground nutmeg 6 ounces potato
1/2 level tsp salt 1 egg

METHOD

Boil the potato. Mash and allow to cool. Beat egg. Sift the flour, nutmeg and salt together into a bowl. Rub in the butter until the mixture resembles breadcrumbs. Add mashed potato and the beaten egg. The dough will be softish and sticky. Roll out on floured surface to 3/4 inch thickness, cut six rounds. You could also use your hands to make round patties with the help of some flour. Place on baking sheet, brush with egg on top and bake for 15 minutes at 350 degrees F.

Non-Vegetarian Variety

Mutton Vindaloo

INGREDIENTS

1/2 kg mutton
1/2 kg potatoes
1/2 kg onions
5-6 red chillies (or according to taste)
10 cloves garlic
1 tbsp finely chopped ginger

1 cup vinegar
4 tbsps vegetable oil
1/2 tsp cumminseed
1/2 inch cinnamon
1 tbsp Worcestershire sauce
3 green chillies
1 tbsp sugar

Method

Wash and cut mutton into bite size pieces. Peel and cut potatotes into large cubes and deep fry to a golden brown colour. Grind together the red chillies, garlic, ginger, cinnamon and cumminseed to a fine paste with the help of half a cup of vinegar.

Put oil in a pan and cook the onions till they are soft and slightly pink. Add the ground spice and sugar and cook together stirring all the time for about five minutes. Add the mutton pieces, stir and cook covered till the liquid from the mutton dries. Then add salt and stir briskly, cooking on high heat for a few minutes. Now add a cup of water, reduce heat and let it simmer till the mutton is tender. Put in the fried potatoes, the rest of the vinegar, the Worcestershire sauce and the finely cut green chillies. Allow it to cook to a boil for just about a minute and serve.

Mutton Chops with Yoghurt

INGREDIENTS

1 kg mutton chops
2 cups natural, unflavoured yoghurt
4 medium sized onions
1 heaped tbsp ginger-garlic paste

1 tbsp garam masala
2 tsps coriander powder
1/2 tsp turmeric
1/2 tsp red chilli powder
3 tbsps vegetable oil
salt to taste

METHOD

Clean and wash mutton. Slice onions lengthwise finely.

Add the spices, the ginger-garlic paste to the yoghurt, mix well and pour over the mutton. Allow to stand for about half an hour. Meanwhile, put the oil and onions in a pan and brown the onions a light golden brown. Add the mutton with the marinade, stir and pressure cook. Add coriander leaves, and decorate with slices of tomato.

Ground Mutton Pie

INGREDIENTS

The potato pastry
2 cups boiled and mashed potato
2 tbsps flour

1 tsps salt
juice of 1 lime
1 egg
4 tbsps butter

The filling

250 gms ground mutton (keema)
1 large onion chopped
3 tbsp oil
1 tsps finely chopped ginger
2 cloves garlic

2 tsps ground pepper
3 eggs
1 cup elbow macaroni, boiled and drained.
salt to taste
1 heaped tsp garam masala

METHOD.

Mix together the ingredients of the potato pastry, using only three tablespoons of butter. Grease a nine inch baking dish with a spoonful of butter. When the pastry is smooth, pat it on to the baking dish, making sure it is even and reaches half way up the sides of the dish. Bake for ten minutes in a preheated oven. (350 degrees).

To make the filling: grind the ginger and garlic together. Put oil, in a pan. When it is hot, add the ginger garlic paste and fry for about thirty seconds. Put in the chopped onion and fry uncovered till it becomes soft and slightly brown.

Now put in the ground mutton. Mix together and cover and cook till the liquid in the mutton is completely absorbed. Add garam masala, black pepper and mix well. Add half a cup of water and cook till mutton is at least three quarters done and is completely dry. Remove from fire and add the macaroni. Let it cool a little before you add the beaten eggs. Then mix in egg to coat the mixture. Pour into baking dish in which the potato pastry was prepared and bake for thirty minutes at 350 degree F. Decorate with grated cheese while still hot and serve immeditely.

Mutton Curry

INGREDIENTS

1/2 kg mutton
1 cup yoghurt, natural, unflavoured
2 large or 3 medium size tomatoes
2 onions finely sliced
1/2 bunch chopped coriander

12-15 peppercorns, freshly roasted and ground
2 tsps cumminseed
2 tsps coriander powder
1 tsp turmeric
1 tsp khus-khus
1 tsp garam masala
2 tbsps cooking oil

METHOD

Prepare the marinade by adding all the spices and the ground ginger to the curds. Mix well, then put in the mutton and using your hands mix the marinade well into the meat. Keep aside for two hours.

Heat the oil and fry the onions to a golden brown. Remove the mutton pieces from the yoghurt and put in the browned onion. Cook slowly, stirring constancy. When the liquid dries up fry for a while, then add the chopped tomatoes. Allow to cook till the tomatoes are softened and their liquid begins to dry up. Then add the yoghurt mixture, stir for a minute to blend the yoghurt and the spices in it. Then add a cup of water and pressure cook till done. Decorate with coriander leaves and sprinkle a little garam masala before serving.

Rich Mutton Mutanjan

INGREDIENTS

Mutton
1/2 kilo mutton
2 large onions
2 half inch pieces
    cinnamon
6 cardamoms
1/2 cup yoghurt
1 tbsp ground ginger
3 cloves garlic
2 green chillies
4 tbsps vegetable oil

Rice
6 cups good quality rice
a few cashewnuts,
pistachios and almonds
1 heaped tbspn raisins
5 tbsp vegetable oil
1/2 kg sugar

METHOD

Clean and wash mutton and cut into bite size pieces. Grind together the onions, green chillies and garlic. Beat the curds.

Mutton : Heat the oil in a pot and put in the ground onions, garlic and green chillies. Brown on a slow flame. Add mutton, two cardamoms, cloves, one piece of cinnamon and the ground ginger. Stir well, allowing the onion and mutton to blend and brown together. Add salt and enough water to cook the mutton.

When the mutton is tender, remove from fire and add the yoghurt. Stir and place back on fire to simmer for five minutes. The mutton should have a little gravy.

Rice : Heat the oil in a thick bottomed pan and fry the rest of the cardamoms in it. Add the washed and drained rice and stir it very gently, allowing the oil to coat all the grains. Then add the exact amount of water required to cook it. (See appendix on cooking rice.)

In a little oil, fry the nuts and raisins and keep aside.

To put it all together: half an hour before serving, lay out half the rice on a serving dish and layer half the mutton over it. Repeat this one more time, leaving about four tablespoons of rice to top over the final mutton layer. Sprinkle nuts and raisins. Bake in pre heated (350) oven for ten minutes and serve.

Mutton Pasanda

INGREDIENTS

500 gms boneless mutton, (preferably mutton leg) cut into minute steak sizes
1 tsp vinegar
2 tsps ginger paste
2 tsps garlic paste
150 gms cashewnuts
50 gms sliced almonds
$1/4$ tsp ground cardamom
$1/4$ tsp clove powder
2 bay leaves
200 gms onion
1 bunch coriander leaves
1 cup oil
salt and pepper

METHOD

Make a mixture of the ginger garlic paste, salt, pepper and vinegar and marinade the chicken in it. Keep aside and prepare the other ingredients.

Chop the onion fine and saute in half the oil till soft and transparent. When cool add to the meat. Allow to marinade another fifteen minutes. Put mutton in a pressure cooker add just half a cup of water and cook till mutton is about three quarters done. Meanwhile, using a little water put in a blender the cashewnuts and mix to a smooth paste. Add the spices: cardamom, cloves, chilli powder. Pour this cashewnuts sauce over the mutton and simmer till meat is well done. Add half the coriander leaves while cooking. When serving, sprinkle the sliced almonds and the rest of the coriander leaves. Plain white rice or chapati goes well with this.

Chicken Royale

INGREDIENTS

1 kilo chicken breast
1/2 kilo potatoes
2 large onions
4 tbsps tomato paste
1 bunch coriander leaves
1 tbsp coriander powder
1 tbsp cummin powder

1/2 cup cottage cheese
1 tbsp tandoori masala
5 cloves garlic
4 cardamoms
1/2 lemon
1 tsp cummin seeds
5 tbsps oil

METHOD

In a large pot put in the oil. Put in the cumminseeds. When they are brown add the diced onions and fry till golden brown. Pour in half a cup of water and when it comes to a boil put in the cleaned, washed, and cut chicken pieces. Stir well and cook for about five minutes. When the liquid has been absorbed, put in the ground garlic, coriander, cummin and tandoori powders, the tomato paste, salt and coriander leaves. Stir for a minute or two, then add two cups of water; cover and cook for ten minutes. Stir occasionally. Add the cubed potatoes. If there is not enough liquid to cook the potatoes, add some water. When the potatoes are ready, add the crumbled cottage cheese and simmer for a few minutes. Curry should have some thick red gravy. Goes well with rice, pita bread and plain paratha.

Chicken Chilli

INGREDIENTS

2 medium size chicken breasts
2 tbsps oil
2 medium onions finely chopped
5 cloves garlic
3 green chillies

2 tsps red chilli powder
1 can whole peeled tomatoes
1 heaped tbsp tomato paste
1 tbsp sugar
2 tsps oregano
2 cups boiled red beans (rajma)

METHOD

In a large pan put in the oil; when hot, put in the onions and cook on medium flame till soft and light brown. Add the chopped green chillies and garlic. Stir for a minute and add the whole peeled tomatoes, chilli powder, oregano and salt. Cover and cook, stirring now and then to help soften and blend the tomatoes into a smooth, thick gravy. Add the tomato paste, stir, cover and allow to simmer for a few minutes.

Put in the chicken, cut into bite size pieces, and the rajma. Stir vigorously, cover and cook on high heat for five minutes, then lower heat and simmer for fifteen minutes allowing the chicken to cook and the flavours to blend. Chicken chilli tastes excellent when eaten with rice, pita bread, chapati, french bread, puri, or poured over a baked potato.

This tomato base is used often for all kinds of pasta, spaghetti, macaroni, lasagna, with generous helpings of cheese on top.

Chicken Palak (Spinach)

INGREDIENTS

1 chicken (about 1/2 kg)
1/2 kilo spinach
1 tsp each, red chilli powder, turmeric, cummin seed
1 inch piece ginger

5 cloves garlic
3 green chillies
2 large onions
4 tbsps oil
salt to taste

METHOD

Clean and joint chicken. Grind to a fine paste: red chillies, ginger, garlic, turmeric, green chillies, cummin. Heat the oil in a saucepan and put in the sliced onions. When they are soft and just beginning to change colour add the ground paste and fry together. Put in the chicken and stir for two minutes. Pour half a cup of water and cook on slow fire. Meanwhile, wash and chop spinach coarsely and boil in its own moisture. Add salt. Grind the spinach and put it in the pan with the chicken. Cook on a high flame and stir briskly. Then reduce flame, cover and lt simmer till chicken is done.

Rich Indian Chicken Curry

INGREDIENTS

1 kg chicken breasts
1/2 kg potatoes
4 tbsps crumbled cottage cheese
2 large onions
4 cloves garlic
1/2 tsp cardamom powder
2 tsps coriander powder

1 heaped tsp cummin seeds
bunch of coriander leaves
3/4 tsp tandoori masala
salt to taste
juice of 1 lemon
4 tbsps cooking oil
2 tbsps tomato paste
1 tbsp red chilli powder

PREPARE AHEAD

Chop onions. Clean and cut chicken into bite size pieces and mix with lemon juice. Peel and cube potatoes. Using half a cup of water blend the tomate paste into a smooth mixture.

METHOD

Put the oil in a pan and when it is hot put in the onions. Cook on medium flame till the onions are a even light brown. Put in the cummin seed and fry together with the onion. Then add the chicken and potatotes. Stir and cover cook for a few minutes allowing the juices of chicken and potatoes to blend and cook together then add the salt, chilli, coriander, tandoori cardamom powders, and half the coriander leaves. Stir well, and put in the chopped garlic and tomato paste. When the liquids have evaporated, add two cups of water. Cover and cook for about five to seven minutes till potatoes are done. Add the cottage cheese and the rest of the coriander leaves. Simmer for two minutes before serving.

Chicken Curry with Cummin

INGREDIENTS

1 kilo boneless chicken
5 tbsps oil
3 heaped tsps cummin seed
2 level tsps coriander powder
1 tsp turmeric
2 tsps chopped ginger

3 green chillies cut fine
4 large tomatoes, chopped
salt to taste
1 tsps cummin powder
big bunch of coriander leaves, chopped
1 tbsp lemon juice

METHOD

Wash the chicken and cut into bite size pieces. Marinate with lemon juice and salt and keep aside for at least half an hour. Heat oil in a saucepan When it begins to smoke, reduce flame and fry the cumminseeds allowing them to brown. Add ginger, green chillies, chicken, coriander leaves and all the dry spices. Mix, then cover and cook on a low flame till all the liquids have dried. Now stir again, making sure the spices are blended in. Add tomatoes and cover. Cook for about ten minutes. Simmer for five minutes. Tastes really good with either plain chapati is or french loaf.

Cheesy Chicken Submarine

INGREDIENTS

2 cups boiled and shredded chicken
1/2 cup mayonnaise
1/2 cup cream cheese
4 tbsps chopped onion
half a bunch chopped coriander leaves
1/2 tsp garlic salt or garlic juice with some salt
1 cup grated cheese
4 tbsps butter
1 French loaf
a few thinly sliced cucumber slices dipped in lemon juice

METHOD

Combine the first seven ingredients blending them with a fork into a smooth spreadable mixture. Cut the french bread lengthwise and butter the lower half. Now spread the chicken mixture. Garnish with the cucumber slices and bake at 450° F for ten minutes. Slice and serve.

Black Pepper Chicken

INGREDIENTS

2 chicken breasts
1 tsp (heaped) ground
   black pepper
6 cardamoms
1/2 tsp salt
1 tbsp oil or butter
2 small tomatoes

1 bunch coriander leaves
1/2 tsp turmeric
1 tsp cumminseed powder
4 cloves garlic
1 tsp chopped ginger
1 tbsp chopped onion
1 tbsp oil or butter

METHOD

Remove skin and as much fat as you can from the chicken breasts. Cut into bite size pieces. Heat oil in pan and put in the cardamoms and then the black pepper. Fry on low flame for about forty-five seconds and then put in the chicken. Add salt, stir well, reduce heat, cover and cook. Stir a few times and cook for about 10 minutes.

    Meanwhile, heat oil in another pan and put in the chopped onion, ginger, garlic. Fry till soft, and add the turmeric, cummin powder and coriander leaves. Stir well and put in the pureed or finely chopped tomatoes. Mix, all cover and cook till the mixture is smooth and well-blended. Now pour the chicken mixture. Add two or three teaspoonfuls of water into the chicken pan to use all of the pepper and cardamom. Stir briskly, add half a cup of water and let it simmer for ten minutes. Serve hot with french bread, chapati, paratha or pita bread.

Egg Vindaloo

INGREDIENTS

8 hardboiled eggs
3 large onions
4 dry red chillies
5 cloves garlic
1 tsp ground ginger
1 tsp cummin powder
3 tbsps oil
2 tomatoes

1/2 inch stick cinnamon
2 green chillies
1 cup vinegar
1 tbsp sugar
1/2 tsp turmeric
1/2 tbsp Worcestshire sauce
salt to taste

METHOD

Shell eggs. Chop onions and tomatoes. Grind red chillies, garlic, ginger, cumminseeds and turmeric in a little vinegar, to a time paste.

Put the oil in a pan and fry the ground spices for two minutes. Add the onions and stir well while cooking. Add the cinnamon stick, green chillies and salt and stir cook till the onions are soft. Now put in the tomatoes and cover and cook for a while, mixing often to blend the gravy to a smooth consistency. Add vinegar, Worcestershire sauce, sugar and stir. Now add the eggs and allow to simmer for a while on a low fire.

Hyderbad Chicken

INGREDIENTS

1 medium sized chicken
100 gms or 4 ozs onion
1 pod of garlic with about 8 to 10 cloves of garlic
1 heaped teaspoon of finely chopped ginger
1 tsp garam masala
1 tsp peanuts
2 tsps desiccated coconut

2 tsps poppy seeds
3/4 cup yoghurt
1 tsp chilli powder
salt
5 green chillies
1 bunch coriander leaves
juice of 1 lemon
3 tbsps oil

METHOD

Grind together : ginger, garlic, coconut, poppy seeds and peanuts. Cut chicken into pieces and rub with lemon juice and salt. Put oil in a pan and heat. Add the chopped onion and cook till light brown. Put in chicken and fry for a while, using the stirring spoon to baste the onion and oil on the chicken pieces while cooking on medium heat. Now add the ground spices and chilli powder. Stir, cover and cook for about 15 to 20 minutes. Finally, add the yoghurt. Mixing it well. Cook till the gravy thickens. Add the chopped coriander leaves, just before serving. This is best served with naan or chapati.

Chinese Prawn Balls

INGREDIENTS

200 gms potatoes
400 gms prawns
2 green chillies
a few spring onions
1 tsp chilli powder

2 eggs beaten
1 tsp ajinomoto
1 cup breadcrumbs
1 tsp oil
oil for deep frying

METHOD

Boil the potatoes and mash till fine. Chop the green chillies and spring onions finely. Chop the prawns coarsely. Heat the oil and fry the spring onions and green chillies for half a minute. Add the chilli powder and fry for half a minute more. Now put in the prawns, salt, ajinomoto, stir and fry for about two to three minutes. Remove from heat, allow to cool for ten minutes and then add the mashed potato. Put in two or three tablespoons of breadcrumbs and mix well. Shape into balls. With greased hands. Dip the balls into beaten egg, toss lightly in breadcrumbs and deep fry till golden brown. This can be eaten with a hot sauce or soya sauce. Makes a good cocktail dish.

Party Prawn Curry

INGREDIENTS

1 kilo prawns
juice of 1 lemon
2 medium sized onions
1 tbsp ginger-garlic paste
1 can coconut milk or 1 1/2
    cups thick cocount milk

3 large tomatoes, chopped fine
3 capsicums cut into small pieces
3 tbsps oil
salt

Spice mixture No. 1

4 tbsps coriander seeds
2 tsps cumminseeds
1 tsp (caraway) jeeri

1 tsp red chilli powder
1 tsp turmeric

Spice mixture No. 2

1 1/2 tsps poppy seeds
    (khus-khus)
1 tsp aniseed (saunf)

5-6 cloves
1 1/2 tbsps desiccated coconut

METHOD

After shelling and deveining the prawns, marinate them with half the ginger-garlic paste, lemon juice and salt for two hours. Fry a few at a time in the oil, removing them as soon as they begin to curl. Fry capsicum similarly. Set both aside. Make the spice mixtures separately by heating the ingredients first on a griddle or tava and then grinding them.

Heat oil, and add onions, and fry till golden brown. Add the second half of the ginger-garlic paste, stir well and add the prawns and capsicum pieces. Mix slowly and put in the first of the ground spice mixtures. When the prawns are almost cooked, add the second spice mixture, the coconut milk and stir for a few minutes. Cover and cook for five minutes. Now add the tomatoes and salt. Cook till the gravy acquires a well blended thick consistency. Decorate with thin lemon slices and serve hot with rice.

Fried Prawn Rice

INGREDIENTS

3 cups long grained rice
200 gms shelled, deveined large size prawns
1/4 cup finely sliced cabbage
1/4 cup shredded carrot
1/2 a capsicum or bell pepper, sliced
1 tbsp vinegar
1 tbsp soya sauce

2 scallions/spring onions chopped
1 tsp red chilli powder
2 cloves garlic
a small piece ginger
1/4 tsp tandoori colour or orange food coloring
1/2 tsp Ajinomoto (MSG)
2 tbsps oil
salt to taste

METHOD

Wash and soak rice for an hour. Wash shelled and deveined prawns and drain. Grind the ginger and garlic together to a fine paste. Cut vegetables.

Heat oil in a pot, till it smokes. Reduce heat and put in the ginger-garlic paste. Stir for about 20 seconds and add the spring onions. Stir and put in the prawns. Stir fry for about two or three minutes, then add the vegetables, salt, red chilli powder, soya sauce, ajinomoto and vinegar. Stir fry this till vegetables are slightly soft (about two or three minutes on medium heat). Now drain, add the rice and mix well for three minutes then pour in 4 cups of water. Now you can turn over the rice into a rice cooker, or just cover and cook till rice is done. As rice qualities vary, the amount of water required for the rice to cook may also vary. If you know that you have a quick cooking rice you may reduce the water to just 3 cups. Later, if more water is needed, add some hot water in small quantities.

Pork Ribs in Sweet and Sour Sauce

INGREDIENTS

6 pork spare ribs
3 tbsps honey
3 tbsps lemon juice

3 tbsps ketchup
2 tbsps oil
salt (optional)

METHOD

In a pot put in all the ingredients, cover with lid and keep on medium heat, till the meat is tender. You may need to stir once or twice to check for tenderness.

This tastes delicious and as you can see is easy to cook. Boneless chicken and chicken leg can also be cooked in this way.

Sri Lankan Fish Curry

INGREDIENTS

4 slices firm fish
1/2 tsp salt
1/4 tsp turmeric
4 tbsps oil
1/4 tsp mustard seed
1/4 tsp cummin
2 medium onions
   sliced

2 cloves garlic, cut fine
small piece ginger, cut fine
2 ground cardamons
a few curry leaves
1 tomato
1 tsp coriander powder
1 tsp red chilli powder
1 cup coconut milk
salt and lemon juice to taste

METHOD

Wash and dry the fish. Marinate with salt and turmeric and keep aside. Put in the oil And in a pan heat. Add mustard seeds and cummin. When the mustard seeds stop popping, put in the onions and cook till soft and lightly browned. Add the tomato and cook for a minute. Then add all the other ingredients and stir well, allowing it to come to a boil. Reduce heat and put in the marinaed fish. Simmer till fish is cooked. Delicious with white rice.

Singapore Noodles

INGREDIENTS

cup rice vermicelli
cup shelled and deveined shrimp
cup diced cooked pork or any meat of your choice

1 small onion sliced
1 green chilli
4 tbspsean sprouts
2 Tbsps oil

For the sauce

1/4 cup chicken stock
1/2 tsp salt
1/4 tsp sugar
1/2 tsp curry powder

2 tbsps oyster sauce
2 tbsps light soya sauc

METHOD

Soak the vermicelli In a pot of hot water for about three minutes. This it a good white gives colour. The drain.

Fry the bean sprouts in a little hot oil for just a minute. Remove from heat, allow some time for the sprouts to veleanse their liquid. Drain whatever excess liquid remains. Now heat a tablespoon of oil in a deep fryer on, a wok if you have one. Put in the green chilli and onions. Stir fry in quick circular motions. Add the shrimp, meat and bean sprouts. Cook till done. Lastly add the vermicelli and mix well. In ix snace in gredients in a small bowl. Add sauce and keep stirring till the sauce is absorbed. Serve hot.

Baked Macaroni and Ham

Ingredients
1 cup elbow macaroni
  boiled al dente
1/2 cup finely chopped
  onion
2 cloves garlic, minced
2 tbsps flour

1 cup milk
1 cup shredded cheddar or
  mozzarella cheese
1 cup cooked ham cut into
  half inch cubes

Half a package of frozen broccoli, thawed. If using fresh broccoli: 6 big florets cut into smaller florets.

1/2 cup soft breadcrumbs
1 tbsps butter or margarine
Preheat the oven to 350° F.

METHOD

Drain the macaroni when done and return it to the pan it was boiled in. Heat two tablespoons of butter and cook the onion and garlic in it till tender and transparent. Reduce heat and stir in the flour, using a wooden spoon. Keep stirring till no lumps remain. Now add all the milk and stir till it bubbles and becomes thick. Put in the cheese and blend in while it melts. Add ham, broccoli and macroni and mix. Pour this into oven proof dish. Dot the top with butter and sprinkle the soft breadcrumbs. Bake in a 350 degree oven for forty minutes. Serve hot.

Vegetarian Delights

Malai Kofta with an Italian Touch

INGREDIENTS

250 gms paneer
1 tbsp finely chopped onion
1 inch piece ginger
3 cloves garlic
4-5 sprigs of coriander leaves
1 tbsp oil
1 tbsp finely powdered almonds

1 slice bread (soaked in water and squeezed out)
1/2 tsp each garam masala, cummin powder, red chilli powder
salt to taste
oil for frying

For the gravy

1 tsp oregano leaves
1 tsp garam masala
1 small onion
1 piece ginger
2 cloves garlic
2 chopped green chillies

1 1/2 cups tomato puree
1/2 cup yoghurt
pepper and salt to taste
2 tbsps oil
grated cheese for garnishing

METHOD

Cut all kofta ingredients fine, mix together and shape into small balls, and deep fry.

To make the gravy: heat the oil in the pan and sold the oregano leaves and garam masala. Fry for a minute, then put in the finely chopped ginger, garlic, onion and green chillies. Fry till onions are just beginning to brown, then pour in the tomato puree and the yoghurt and add pepper and salt. Allow to simmer till well blended. Add half a cup of water and cook covered for ten minutes. Place the paneer koftas in a bake-proof serving dish and pour the gravy over it. Decorate with cheese, and bake for fifteen minutes at 300 degrees F.

Paneer Cashewnut Curry

INGREDIENTS

400 gms paneer
2 cups green peas
1 cup cashewnuts
1 tsp cummin powder
1 tsp chilli powder
3 green chillies
1 tsp garam masala

1 large or 2 small onions sliced
4 medium sized tomatoes
2 tbsps tomato paste
3 tbsps oil
salt to taste

METHOD

Grind the cashewnuts, slice the onions and chop the tomatoes. Blen the tomato paste. In a spoonful of water. In a saucepan pour the oil and Put in the onions. Saute them till they turn pink. Now add all the ingredients, except the paneer and peas. Cook together for a few minutes, then put off the fire, wait for gravy to cool and pass it through a blender to make a paste. Add two cups of water to this, put it back in the saucepan and bring it to a boil. Boil for five minutes on reduced flame, then put in the paneer and peas. When the peas are done, simmer for a few more minutes. Gravy should be plentiful but thick. Decorate with coriander leaves when serving.

Cauliflower Spinach Sukha

INGREDIENTS

1 large cauliflower
500 gms spinach (palak)
7 cloves of garlic
spring onions
4 green chillies
1 tbsp ground ginger
1/4 tsp asafoetida

1/2 tsp turmeric
2 tsps cummin powder
2 tsps mango powder
(amchoor)
    or lemon juice
salt to taste
3 tbsps oil
tomato slices for garnishing

METHOD

Cut the cauliflower into medium size flowerets. Chop the washed and cleaned spinach finely. Cut ginger, garlic, green chillies and spring onions finely too. Heat the oil in a pan and put in spring onions. Stir well. Cook on a lowish flame. If the liquid from the spinach is not sufficient for cooking the cauliflower, add a little water. Serve garnished with tomato slices.

Mushrooms Au Gratin

INGREDIENTS

400 gms fresh or
   canned mushrooms
3 tbsps butter
2 tbsps flour
1/2 cup milk

1 cup sour cream
salt, black pepper
2 tbsps grated Parmesan
   cheese
1 bell pepper or capsicum
   (optional)

METHOD

Slice the mushrooms finely and saute in the butter for about six to eight minutes. Gently sprinkle the flour and cook for another five minutes, stirring all the time. Keep ready the sour cream mixed with the milk to which the salt, pepper and lemon juice has been added. Add the mushrooms to this mixture. Pour into a greased, flat ovenproof dish. Decorate with cirles of bell pepper, than sprinkle the Parmes an cheese and bake at $375°$ F.for about twenty minutes or until the top is lightly brown. Oven should be preheated.

Instant Lasagna

INGREDIENTS

6 strips of lasagna
300 gms can of cream of celery soup
300 gms package of frozen cut broccoli
1/4 cup vinegar mixed with 1 tbsps sugar

1 tbsp dried oregano
1/2 bunch or 1/2 cup chopped coriander leaves
200 gms shredded Swiss cheese
200 gms cooked, ground chicken (optional for vegetarians)
3/4 cup water

METHOD

Put together the soup, broccoli, vinegar, oregano and heat together to make a smooth sauce. Using a glass oven proof dish arrange the first layer of lasagna, uncooked. Sprinkle half the cheese, then put half the the chicken and then spoon the sauce over it. Repat this layer on more time. Around the edge of the dish pour the water then cover securely with tin foil. Bake in a 350° degree oven for about an hour or till the lasagna noodles are tender.

Party Vegetarian Lasagna

INGREDIENTS

9 packaged lasagna strips, boiled al dente and unbroken.
1 large can tomatoes, pureed
4 large tomatoes, pureed
2 onions, chopped
6 cloves garlic
4 tbsps oil
4 green chilies
1 bunch coriander leaves (cilantro)

2 cups crumbled paneer
1 cup shredded mozzarella
2 cup chopped mushrooms
1 Tbsp oregano
salt to taste
2 Tbs lemon juice
1 Tbsp sugar
2 tsps garam masala
4 bay leaves
1 tsp level red chilli powder
1 tsp cummin seed powder

METHOD

This is a three layered lasagna dish baked in a 12"x 8" pyrex dish. Since lasagna does tend to break while boiling I always boil about eleven or twelve strips so that I can 'repair' the broken strips to make complete layers.

Each layer of lasagna is topped by three layers of stuffing.

Topping 1. Tomato

Chop garlic and green chilies and cook in a pan with three tablespoons of oil. When soft and slightly browned, add one onion and the bay leaves and cook gently, stirring to blend. Add oregano, most of the coriander leaves (leave some for garnishing the topmost layer) and stir for about two minutes.

Then add all the tomatoes, required salt and cover and cook, stirring occasionally. The sauce is done when it is smooth and thick. It should be about two cups.

Topping 2. Mushroom.

Heat one tablespoon of oil and when it heats add a teaspoon of black pepper. Then add the rest of the chopped onion and cook gently till soft and lightly brown. Add the mushrooms, salt and garam masala and stir well. Cover and cook for about two minutes. Then add half a cup of water and bring to a boil and simmer for five minutes.

Topping 3. Crumbled paneer mixed with the teaspoon of cummin seed powder and mozzarella.

To put it all together: grease the baking dish and spread two tablespoons of tomato mixture at the base. Arrange three strips of lasagna in a layer lengthwise on the dish. Now add another two teaspoons on top of the lasagna spreading it evenly. Put a layer of cooked mushroom next and then add the crumbled panner. Only a little of the mozzarella has to be spread in this first round. Continue the second round of layering. Spread a major part of the mozzarella in the final round, garnigh decorate with the coriander leaves and bake in a 350 degree oven for forty-five minutes. Serve hot with crisp garlic bread which can be put in the oven along with the lasagna, for the last fifteen minutes. You can keep the lasagna layered and ready to bake in the freezer for at least a week. It is a great stand by for sudden dinner guests.

Fettuchini Alfredo

Fetuccini : Long flat spaghetti

There are many recipes for this all time Italian favourite. The one here is enjoyed by children and adults alike. It makes a filling healthy main dish and is a quick preparation. It is important to prepare this just before eating.

INGREDIENTS

About 10-12 cups water
1 tsp salt
1 tbsp cooking oil
500 gms pack of Fettuchini
1/2 cup quartered
   button mushrooms

1/2 cup Parmesan cheese
1/3 cup light cream
freshly ground black pepper
3 tbsps butter or margarine

METHOD

Boil the water in a big pot, allowing plenty of room for the fettuchini to cook. Add oil to the water and slowly put in the fettucini. Add a little at a time so that the water continues to maintain even temperature, then reduce heat and continue boiling. Cook uncovered and stir occasionallly. In the meantime, saute the mushrooms in one tablespoon of butter.

Pasta should be strained when it is almost, not completely, done. This is called al dente. Drain right away. Do not rinse the fettucini in cold water. When completely drained, put it back in the pot (still warm) in which it was boiled. Now add the Parmesan cheese, sauteed mushroom, cream and two tablespoons butter or margarine. Put back on very low flame and toss gently till the pasta is well coated. Serve on a warmed dish with fresh pepper sprinkled on top.

Brinjal Curry

INGREDIENTS

400 gms brinjals
1 heaped tsp coriander powder
1 tbsp poppy seed
1 tbsp desiccated coconut
salt and red chilli powder to taste

a pinch of turmeric
4 tbsps tamarind juice
200 gms onion
2 pods garlic
1 tsp ground ginger
lemon juice to taste
5 tbsps oil

METHOD

Wash and dry brinjals then slit them lengthwise without cutting them. Combine the salt, red chilli powder and turmeric and apply to the brinjals. Keep aside to marinate while the other ingredients are prepared.

Grind the poppy seeds and desciccated coconut. Slice the onions finely and fry in two tablespoons of oil. When the onion is a even golden colour, add the garlic and cook for a minute. Now remove from fire and allow to cool. Grind the fried onion and garlic. Grind the ginger, coriander, green chillies and half the coriander leaves with it. Fry this mixture in about two tablespoons of oil. Add the desiccated coconut mixture in it and fry. Remove from pan. Add the rest of the oil (one tablespoon) to the pan and fry the brinjals. When the brinjals are well fried add the mixture, stirring well. Now put in the tamarind juice and half a cup of water. Cover and cook on a medium fire allowing it to simmer. Serve with the rest of the coriander leaves sprinkled on top.

Greek Macaroni Salad

INGREDIENTS

1/2 cup macaroni
1 cup fresh spinach
2 cherry tomatoes
1/2 cup black olives
1/2 cup feta cheese
   or paneer

1 tbsp olive oil or salad oil
2 tbsps vinegar
1 tsp dried oregano
1/2 tsp ground black pepper

METHOD

Break the long macaroni into one inch even pieces and boil in salted water. Remove al dente and rinse in cold water. Drain.

   Keep ready : Spinach torn, not cut. Cut tomatoes in quarters. Cheese or paneer Crumble. Oilves Slice.

   To put it all together: In a medium size salad bowl, preferably glass or wood, put in the pasta, spinach, tomatoes, olives and cheese/paneer. Toss to mix. Make the dressing by putting the oil, vinegar, oregano and pepper in a blender. You can also use a bottle with a tight top and shake well to blend. Pour the dressing on the salad and toss till all ingredients are well coated. Cover with plastic wrap and chill. Allow flavours to blend. Three hours of chilling gives best results.

Fruity Cabbage Salad

INGREDIENTS

1 can pineapple chunks (8 ozs)
1 medium banana sliced
3 cups finely shredded cabbage
1 cup thinly sliced celery
1 cup mandarin oranges, sectioned
1/2 cup walnuts
1 tbsp lemon Juice
1 small container orange yoghurt
1/4 cup raisins
1/2 tsp salt

METHOD

Drain pineapple, reserving only two tablespoons of the syrup. Combine the two tablespoons of pineapple juice and lemon juice and toss banana slices in it. Store the juice for use later. In a large bowl, put in the cabbage, banana, celery, nuts and raisins. Add the juice To the yoghurt and half a teaspoon salt and blend well. Pour on cabbage mixture, toss to coat, cover and chill or at least two hours before eating.

Sauteed Mushrooms

INGREDIENTS

2 cups fresh or canned button mushrooms chopped in quarters
2 cloves garlic made fine in a blender
1 shallot chopped
2 tbsps oil or butter
1 tbsp lemon juice

1/2 cup bread crumbs
1/2 cup grated Parmesan cheese
2 tbsps finely chopped parsley
salt and freshily ground pepper

METHOD

Saute the garlic and the shallots in the oil or butter on a gentle fire for about a minute, stirring all the time with a wooden spoon and mashing the garlic and shallot to a fine consistency. Add the quartered mushrooms and stir. Cover and cook for about eight minutes, strring occasionally stirring. Add lemon juice and salt and stir for a mintue more. Add bread, cheese, and pepper and serve immediately.

Sauteed dishes cook well in a deep frying pan like a wok or the Indian karaie. This is a quick preparation and comes in useful when you discover that one of the guests at dinner is a vegetarian. This is a good accompanying dish for non-vegetarians as well.

Quick Cook Dal-Cha

INGREDIENTS

2 potatoes
2 eggplants
2 tomatoes
2 green chillies
2 red chillies (a variety of green chilli which comes in this colour)
1/2 cup "dal"
1 heaped tsp coriander seeds
1 heaped tsp cummin seeds
1 heaped tsp caraway seeds (zeeri)
5 dried red chillies
1/2 tsp turmeric
1 tbsp ginger
handful of green onion
2 cloves garlic
2-2 1/2 cups light tamarind water
salt to taste
5 tbsps oil

METHOD

Cut potatoes, eggplant and tomatoes into small pieces. Slit the green and red chillies lengthwise. Boil dal and grind. Make a curry paste by grinding together coriander, cummin and caraway seeds, the dry chillies, turmeric and ginger. Finely slice the green onion and garlic.

Fry the onions and garlic in oil till soft, add the curry paste and stir and cook it for five minutes, then put in the dal and potatoes. When the potatoes are half cooked put in the eggplant and tomatoes, salt and the tamarind water. Bring it to a boil at a high heat, then reduce fire and let it simmer till cooked. Vegetables must remain firm. Good accompaniment to plain white rice.

Cabbage Cutlets

INGREDIENTS

1 medium head of cabbage
2 large or 3 medium potatoes boiled and mashed
1/2 tsp ginger
2 tbsps onion
juice of 1 lemon
4 green chillies
salt to taste
half a bunch of coriander leaves
oil to fry

METHOD

Gently separate cabbage leaves from head without breaking. Put a cup of water in a pan, add salt and put in the leaves to steam for ten minutes.

Grind the onion, chilli and ginger together. Put a tablespoon of oil in a pan and heat. Then add the ground mixture and fry for a minute. Put in the mashed potato and stir well for about two minutes on medium heat.

Spread a thin layer of potato mixture on each cabbage leaf and roll gently. Dip each roll in either beaten egg or a thin-non given in ingredients mixture of flour and water and roll again in breadcrumbs. Deep fry till golden brown. Garnish with coriander leaves or slices of capsicum.

Green Peas and Cashewnut Curry

INGREDIENTS

250 gms small round potatoes peeled
oil for deep frying
an additional 2 tbsps of oil
half a cup shelled green peas
250 gms yoghurt
250 gms paneer
6 green chillies chopped fine
15 gms cashewnuts chopped
salt to taste
a handful of chopped fresh coriander leaves

For the curry paste

1 inch piece of cinnamon
2 cardamoms, seeds only
3 cloves
6 black peppercorns
2 dry red chillies
1/2 tsp cumminseed
1/2 tsp coriander seeds
1 tsp poppy seeds (khus-khus)
1 inch piece fresh ginger

METHOD

Prick each potato with a fork two or three times and deep fry till slightly browned and done. Drain and keep warm. Boil the peas in just enough water for it to be cooked, drain and set aside. You do not need to do this if using frozen peas. Set the oven to preheat at 350 degrees or gas mark 4. To make the paste; blend of the curry paste all the ingredients using a little water to make it fine and smooth. Heat the two tablespoons of oil in a pot, put in the paste and cook uncovered for two minutes. Add yoghurt and cook a little more, stirring now and then. Pour half the cooked paste in a baking dish, add half the potatoes, peas and cubed or crumbled paneer. Sprinkle some green chillies and chopped nuts. Now pour the second half of the cooked paste and add rest of the potatoes, peas and paneer. Sprinkle salt, a little more green chillies, nuts and coriander leaves and bake for fifteen minutes.

This is a rich mughlai vegetable which goes well either with parathas or plain rice.

Seyal Cheese Macaroni Bake

INGREDIENTS

2 cups boiled macaroni
2 large tomatoes
2 onions
1 1/2 cups grated cheese
1/2 tin evaporated milk
1 inch piece ginger
4 cloves of garlic
3 green chillies

half a bunch of coriander leaves
a tsp each of cummin, coriander and red chilli powder
5 tbsps tomato ketchup
1 tsp cumminseeds
3 tbsps oil

METHOD

Put the oil in a pan and keep on fire. When the oil is hot reduce that fire and put in the cumminseeds. As soon as the seeds begin to brown, add the ground ginger, garlic and chopped chillies. Fry for a few minutes and then put in the chopped onions. When the onions are soft and slightly brown, add the pureed tomatoes and all the dry powders. Stir and cook till well blended. Now put in the macaroni (which should be slightly underboiled), stir for just a minute, then cover and put off the fire. Allow to cool for about half an hour. Add ketchup, the coriander leaves (keep some for garnishing), the evaporated milk and grated cheese. Mix well, then pour into baking dish and bake at 300 degrees for thirty minutes. Serve hot. Popular with both adults and children and a complete meal.

Goanese Potatoes

INGREDIENTS

1/2 grated coconut
2 onions
10 dried red chillies
2 tsp coriander seeds
2 tsp khus-khus
3 cloves, 1/2 inch stick of cinnamon and a few peppercorns
10 cloves garlic
1 kilo potatoes
4 large tomatoes
1 cup boiled peas
4 tbsps oil
salt to taste

METHOD

Put the oil in a pan and fry the cinnamon, khus-khus, coriander seeds, ginger, garlic, red chillies and grated coconut for just about two minutes and then grind them all into a fine paste. Put the onions, skin and all, directly on the fire. When the skin turns all black, remove from fire, peel off the skin and grind the rest of the onion into a fine paste. Cut tomatoes and cook in about a cup of water, till it becomes a sauce. Saute the peeled and cubed potatoes in a spoonful of oil. You now have the dry spices ground, the onion ground, the tomatoes made into a sauce and the potatoes sauteed. Put the last tablespoon of oil in a pan and fry the onion paste till lightly brown, add the spice paste and cook together, stirring all the time. Now add the tomato sauce, peas and potatoes, cover and cook. Cheese and coriander leaves make a good garnishing.

Sukha Okra

INGREDIENTS

20 tender
okra (bhindi)
1/2 tsp salt

1/2 tsp each of cummin seed, coriander, black pepper powder and amchoor.
1 tbsp oil

METHOD

Wash okra and drain rightaway. Pat dry with paper towel. Clip off head and tail of okra and cut into half inch rounds. Keep everything dry: knife, chopping board, - this helps to keep the okra from getting sticky and unmanageable. In a pan, heat oil and put in all the okra, add all the spices. Cover and cook. Do not stir. You may hold the pan and toss the okra, though this does not have to be done till it is ready to be served.

Sukha Eggplant

INGREDIENTS

2 eggplants
oil for deep frying
powdered spices : cummin, coriander, red chilli, black pepper, salt, amchoor. A tsp of each mixed together.

METHOD

Cut the eggplant into pieces, each about three inches in length and about a quarter inch thick. Make two or three shallow gashes on both sides of the eggplant strips. Soak in salt water for half an hour and then drain. Deep fry till brown. Sprinkle the powdered spices and serve.

Capsicum Pulao

INGREDIENTS

4 cups good quality rice
3 capsicums
2 onions
1 1/2 tsps each of the
    following powders:
coriander, cummin,
turmeric, chilli,
garam masala

1 tbsp lemon juice
salt
10 gms each raisins and
cashewnuts
5 tbsps oil

METHOD

Clean rice, wash and drain well. Cut capsicums into four lengthwise and then each strip into two breath wise. Heat three tablespoons of oil in a pan and fry sliced onions till soft and evenly light brown. Add all dry powders, salt and lime juice. Mix and add the capsicum; then five tablspoons of water to blend the spices. Remove and keep aside. Using the same pan, put in the rest of the oil, fry the raisins and cashews and keep aside. Now put in the rice and gently stir fry for about five minutes, then add three and a half cups of water, cover and cook till the water is all absorbed and the rice is almost done. Pour the capsicum mixture over the-rice, stir just once. Cover tightly and cook on slow fire. Decorate with raisins and cahewnuts before serving.

Potatoes in Green Gravy

INGREDIENTS

500 gms potatoes
2 medium onions
1 bunch coriander leaves
2 tsps dry fenugreek leaves or half a bunch fresh leaves (methi)
2 sprigs spinach
4 green chillies
10 cloves garlic
ginger: enough to make a heaped teaspoon when ground
4 tomatoes
4 tbsps oil
1 tsps turmeric
salt

METHOD.

Chop finely the coriander, fenugreek and spinach leaves the green chillies, garlic, ginger and onions. Put in a pan, and add the dry spices, turmeric, salt and coriander powder. Add the finely chopped tomatoes. Using, your hands, in a kneading action mix all these ingredients together. Add oil, then cover and cook till it is cooled and the oil surfaces. Add the cubed and potatoe mix well so that the gravy reaches all the potatoes. Add enough water for the potatoes to cook and still leave you with some gravy. This gravy is a Sindhi favourite. It is a good base for fish, prawns, okra, and peas with paneer. Enjoyable with chapati or rice.

Indonesian Curry

INGREDIENTS

12 red chillies
2 cloves garlic
25 small red onions
10-12 string beans
1 large or two small potatoes
1 egg plant
1 small cabbage

2 small carrots
2 tsps chopped ginger
1 tsp turmeric
1 cup coconut milk, canned or fresh
5/6 cardamoms
2 tbsps cooking oil
salt to taste

METHOD

Make a paste by grinding together the red chillies, onions, garlic. Clean the string beans and cut them into two. Cut the potatoes, carrot and eggplant into cubes. Chop cabbage into larg pieces. In a pan put in the oil and heat. When it begins to smoke, reduce flame and put in the cardamoms. Fry gently for a minute and add the ground paste. Fry again for a few minutes. Put in all the vegetables, add salt and turmeric, stir, cover and cook for two minutes. Put in the ginger and stir gently, but well. The mixture will be completely dry at this point. Put in a cup of water, and allow it to come to a boil. When the vegetables are almost ready, add the coconut milk. Stir well. If you need more gravy you will need to add some water. This curry is pretty hot and balances well with rice.

Ginger-flavoured Cauliflower

This is a dry curry suitable for eating with Indian breads such as chapati or paratha. It also serves as a good stuffing for pita.

INGREDIENTS

1/2 kg cauliflower
1 tsp ground ginger
2 tbsps cooking oil
1 tsp coriander powder
1 tsp cumminseed powder

red chilli powder to taste or chopped green chilli,
salt
2 medium sized tomatoes (about 100 gms)
1 tsp lemon juice

METHOD

Prepare ahead. Cut cauliflower into flowerettes. Wash and drain. Chop tomatoes into small pieces or use blender to grind into a fairly smooth puree.

Keep pan on fire and add the oil. When it begins to smoke, reduce heat and add the ginger. Cook on slow flame for about half a minute, then add the cauliflower, coriander and cumminseed powder, tomato, salt, red chilli powder or the green chillies. Cover and cook on medium heat for about fifteen minutes. Stir and cook covered till cauliflower is as soft as you personally prefer it. Add lemon juice before serving and sprinkle a little cumminseed powder when it is on the serving dish. A little red chill powder sprinkled on top also adds some colour.

Cauliflower Spinach Sukha

INGREDIENTS

1 large cauliflower
300 gms spinach (palak)
7 cloves of garlic
7 sprigs of spring onion
4 green chillies
1 tbsp ground ginger
1/4 tsp asafoetida

1/2 tsp turmeric
2 tsps cummin powder
1 tsp mango powder
   (amchoor) or lemon juice
salt to taste
3 tbsps oil
tomato slices for garnishing

METHOD

Cut the cauliflower into medium size flowerets. Wash and chop the spinach finely. In a food processor put in the garlic, green chillies, ginger and spring onions and chop till fine but not a paste. Heat oil in a pan put the asafoetida, fry for just a few seconds (asafoetida fries very quickly), then add the chopped garlic ginger mixture. Put in the chopped spinach & cook covered for five minutes, then add the cauliflower, turmeric, cummin powder.

Mushroom with Yoghurt

INGREDIENTS

250 gms fresh button mushrooms or 2 cans of button mushrooms
1 medium size onion chopped
1/2 cup paneer
1/2 cup yoghurt
5 green chillies
2 inch piece of ginger and 10 cloves of garlic (ground to a paste)
4 chopped tomatoes
2 tbsps coconut powder
1 tsp cummin
1 tsp garam masala
1 tsp red chilli powder
3/4 tsp turmeric
1 bunch coriander leaves
4 tbsps oil
salt to taste

METHOD

Wash mushrooms well and cut into quarters. Heat the oil in a pan and fry the cummin seeds till brown, add the onion, stir well for two minutes then put in the ginger-garlic paste and the green chillies. Stir fry until the mixture is soft. Put in the chopped tomatoes and all the spices. Cover and cook, mixing now and then. When the gravy starts to leave the sides of the pan or the tomatoes are softened and well blended into a gravy, add the yoghurt. When it is ready the oil will surface. Put in mushrooms and cook on low flame for about fifteen minutes or till mushrooms are done. Remove pan from fire, add the crumbled paneer and mix together. Serve decorated with coriander leaves.

Cabbage Manchurian

INGREDIENTS

1 medium sized cabbage, chopped very fine in blender or grated
1 tsp ginger-garlic paste
2 tsps soya sauce
1 tsp Ajinomoto (monosodium glutamate, also called Accent)
4 tsps cornflour
2 tsps plain flour
2 tsps black pepper powder
4 green chillies, chopped fine
salt to taste
oil for deep frying

For coating

5 tsps cornflour

For the sauce

2 tsps ginger garlic-paste
2 tsps cornflour mixed with two tbsps of water
2 green chillies chopped fine
2 tsps soya sauce
A pinch of salt, Ajinomoto and sugar
1 tsp black pepper powder
2 tsps oil

METHOD

To make the cabbage balls, mix the ingredients together and then divide them into small portions and shape them into balls. Make a mixture of cornflour and four tablespoons of water. Coat each ball with it and deep fry.

To make the sauce. Fry the ginger garlic paste in two

teaspoon of oil. Add green chillies, soya sauce, cornflour mixture, salt, sugar, Ajinomoto and black pepper. When the gravy is smooth and thick, add the cabbage balls. Cover and simmer for five minutes before serving.

Macaroni Mushroom Bake

INGREDIENTS

3 cups boiled elbow macaroni
2 tbsps plain flour
3 tbsps margarine
2 cups milk
1 can milk

1 can mushrooms
1/2 can mushroom soup
1/2 onion chopped
1/2 cup grated cheese
salt, black, pepper, coriander leaves

METHOD

Using half the margarine, saute the onions and keep aside. Make white sauce in another pan, keeping the fire low at all times. Put the rest of the margarine in a pan and when it melts add the flour. Stir this so it does not brown but gets evenly cooked (about one minute). Then pour the milk, keep stirring continuously, till it becomes thick and has the consistency of tomato sauce. Add pepper, salt, fried onion, then the sliced mushrooms, mushroom soup and macaroni. Mix all together then pour into a greased baking dish, garnish with cheese and coriander leaves and bake in a preheated oven (350 F) for thirty minutes.

Potato and Eggplant Curry

INGREDIENTS

4 medium potatoes
2 large or 4 long, skinny eggplants
1 tbsp finely minced ginger
4 green chillies

1 1/2 tsps coriander powder
1 tsp turmeric
4 medium tomatoes
3 tbsps vegetable oil
salt to taste
half a bunch coriander leaves

Prepare ahead

Peel and cut potatoes in one inch cubes. Cut eggplant length wise into four quarters, then cut again into inch cubes. Cut ginger, tomatoes, green chillies and coriander leaves.

METHOD

Put the pan on medium heat and pour in three tablespoons of oil. When it begins to smoke, reduce heat and put in the ginger and green chillies. Cook for half a minute on low heat. Add the potatoes, cover and cook for three minutes. Now add the eggplant and dry spices and stir gently. Put in tomatoes and coriander leaves, cover and cook on low heat till potatoes are done.

Cheese Kofta Curry

INGREDIENTS

For the kofta

4 medium sized boiled potatoes (about 450 gms)
100 gms grated cheese
1 small onion finely chopped
1 cup chopped cabbage

1-2 tsp salt or to taste
half a bunch of coriander leaves chopped.
3 slices of bread
1 tsp cummin powder
1 tsp lemon juice or amchoor

For the curry

5 tbsps oil
5-6 curry leaves
1 tsp cumminseed
4 tomatoes (about 400 gms)
1 inch or 1 heaped tsp of grated ginger
1 tsp grated or finely chopped garlic
1 tsp chilli powder

1 tsp each of cummin powder, coriander powder and turmeric
2 tbsps tomato ketchup
2 tsp yoghurt
2 tbsps coconut,
1 tbsp poppy seeds
1 tbsp sesame seeds
3 cloves
2 cardamons ground together.

METHOD

Koftas

Mix all kofta ingredients together. Bread can be added in

either of two ways: (a) soak in water for two minutes, then squeeze out all the water using both hands and put the dry, damp bread in the kofta mixture, or (b) put the fresh or day old bread in the blender and run it till it becomes fine, soft crumbs and add it to the kofta mixture. Mix well, then make into round or oval patties and deep fry. Keep aside to use just before serving.

Curry

Heat the five tablespoons of oil in a pan and put in the chopped garlic, ginger and cummin first. When brown add tomato ketchup, salt, all the dry spices and cook for a minute. Then add the yoghurt and the ground spices. Cook till the oil floats surface. Add two cups of water and let it simmer for about fifteen minutes till the spices are all cooked and well blended into a smooth, thick gravy.

To serve, arrange the koftas in a flat serving dish and pour the hot gravy over it. Garnish with some coriander leaves (These ingredients make about 25 koftas).

Peas Mushroom Curry

INGREDIENTS

1 cup peas (fresh or frozen)
1 cup quartered white or button mushrooms (fresh or canned)
2 tbsps oil
1 heaped tsp cummin seed
1 level tsp turmeric
1 tsp coriander powder
1 tsp salt or to taste
1 tsp chopped ginger
2 green chillies chopped fine
2 small tomatoes chopped or pureed in blender
1/2 bunch chopped coriander leaves

METHOD

Put the oil in a pot and keep it on the fire. When the oil begins to smoke, reduce heat and put in the cummin seeds allowing them to fry gently till brown. Add all the other ingredients, stir, cover and cook for three minutes on a high flame. Stir again for a minute or two, reduce heat and cook covered for about ten minutes.

The curry is done when the oil surfaces. However, the oil in these recipes have been kept to a minimum and there may not be enough oil to surface. It makes sense, health-wise, to keep the oil down and forego the luxury of having it. The curry is done when the tomatoes and the spices have blended smoothly

Baked Vegetable Casserole

INGREDIENTS

2 large potatoes
2 carrots
1/2 cup peas
1/2 cup boiled macaroni
1/2 tsp ground ginger
1/2 tsp ground garlic

red chilli powder or Paprika
salt to taste
2 tsps butter or margarine
1/2 cup milk
1 tsp lemon juice

METHOD

Boil and dice potatoes. Clean carrots, dice and boil in half a cup of water with a little salt. Drain.

Heat two teaspoons butter or margarine in a pan. When the butter begins to smoke, reduce the heat and add garlic and ginger. Stir a few times, then add all the vegetables, macaroni and the chopped coriander leaves. Add salt, lemon juice and red chilli powder. Stir very gently, or hold the pot on either side and gently move it. The vegetables and spices must blend but not break. Add the milk and bake for thirty minutes in a preheated oven at 350 degrees Fahrenheit.

Spicy Mixed Vegetable Pie

INGREDIENTS

1/2 cup beans
1/2 cup carrots
1/2 cup cauliflower
1 large capsicum
1/2 cup grated cheese
1/2 cup breadcrumbs
1 tsp ground ginger
1/2 cup peas

salt to taste
1 tsp coriander powder
1 bunch coriander leaves
1 tsp cumminseed powder
1/2 tsp black pepper
1 egg (optional)
3 tbsps cooking oil

METHOD

Wash and drain peas. Cut beans finely. Chop carrots into quarter inch cubes. Cut capsicum into circles and chop coriander leaves.

In a pot put the oil and keep it on medium heat. When it heats, add the teaspoonful of ginger. After about ten seconds, add all the prepared vegetables except capsicum and bread crumbs Keep aside some coriander leaves for later. Add salt, black pepper, coriander and cummin seed powders and stir well. Add half a cup of water, cover and cook for about ten minutes. Allow the vegetables to cool. In a baking dish arrange a layer of vegetables, then sprinkle cheese. Repeat these layers. Decorate the top with circles of capsicum and cheese. Bake for thirty minutes on 350 degree Fahrenheit. After the oven is turned off, sprinkle the bread crumbs and allow the dish to stay in the oven for ten minutes. Remove, add the coriander leaves and serve hot. Serves four.

If you are using egg it must be added to the cooked vegetables just before pouring into the baking dish.

Spinach Mushroom Bake

INGREDIENTS

600 gms spinach
1 can cream of mushroom soup
1 cup boiled elbow macaroni
1 tsp ground ginger
1 tsp ground garlic
1 cup capsicum, cut into circles

1/2 cup coarsely grated carrot
1/2 cup onion chopped fine
3 large tomatoes chopped
1 cup grated mozzarella cheese
3 green chillies
salt to taste

METHOD

Put the washed and cut spinach in a pot along with chopped green chillies, ginger, garlic, tomatoes and salt. Cook till all the liquid has evaporated and the spinach is soft. Run through a blender to get an even puree. Pour into the pot. Add the mushroom soup and mix well. Put in the boiled macaroni and mix again.

Preheat oven to 400 degrees F. Butter a glass baking dish and pour half the spinach mixture in it. Spread a layer of grated carrot and capsicum and then half the cheese. Pour the remaining spinach and repeat the layers.

Bake for first 20 minutes at 400 degrees F, then reduce the heat to 350 degrees F. Allow to bake for 30 minutes. Cheese should be a nice golden brown. This makes a very delicious entrèe.

Cakes & Desserts

Russian Tea-Cakes

INGREDIENTS

1 cup butter or margarine
1 cup icing sugar
1/2 cup confectioner's sugar
1 tsp vanilla
1 cup all-purpose flour
1/4 tsp salt
1/2 cup finely chopped nuts

METHOD

Heat oven to 400 degrees F. Mix the butter (or margarine) and sugar together. Add vanilla. Work in flour, salt and nuts until dough holds together. Shape dough into 1 inch balls. Place on ungreased baking dish.

Bake for about 12 minutes or until set but not brown. While warm, roll in confectioner's sugar. When cool, roll in the sugar once more.

Do not substitute self-raising flour for all-purpose flour.

Carrot Cake

INGREDIENTS

1 1/4 cups sugar
1 1/2 cups shredded carrots
1 1/2 cups water
1 cup raisins
1 tbsp butter or margarine
1/2 tsp ground cloves
1 tsp ground cinnamon and nutmeg
2 1/2 cups self-raising flour
1 tsp bicarbonate of soda
1/2 tsp salt
1 cup chopped nuts
sifted icing sugar (optional)

METHOD

In a large pan put together sugar, carrots, water, raisins, butter, cinnamon, nutmeg and cloves. Stir and heat this mixture slowly until it simmers. Stir till sugar has dissolved completely. Allow to simmer on gentle flame for about five minutes. Remove the pan from the fire and stand this mixture at room temperature overnight. The next day beat in the flour, soda and salt in this mixture until blended. Fold in nuts. Spoon in mixture into nine-inch floured cake tin or ring. Bake at 150 degrees C for about one hour and forty-five minutes. Cake is done when a toothpick inserted in the centre of the cake comes out clean. Let the cake cool in the tin for five minutes, then turn out and cool completely. Sprinkle all over with icing sugar before serving.

Nutritious Oatmeal Biscuits

INGREDIENTS

185 gms butter (6 ozs)
1 tightly packed cup of
   brown sugar
1/2 cup white sugar
1 egg
1 tbsp water
1 tsp vanilla essence

2/3 cup plain flour
1 tsp ground cinnamon
1/2 tsp bicarbonate of soda
1/2 tsp salt
3 cups quick oats
1 cup sultanas or chocolate
   bits

METHOD

Beat together butter and sugar until fluffy. Add the egg, water and essence and continue beating. Sift together the flour, cinnamon, soda and salt. Stir this into the egg and sugar mixture, mixing well. Fold in the oats and either the sultanas or the chocolate bits. Drop level tablespoons on greased baking trays, leaving room for spreading. Bake for 15-17 minutes or till the edges are browned. Centres remain soft and crumbly. Cool and store.

Basic Muffins

INGREDIENTS

2 cups plain white flour or
1 cup each of wheat flour and plain flour
1 egg
3/4 cup milk
1/2 cup sugar

1/2 cup vegetable oil or stick of margarine
3 tsps baking powder
1 level tsp salt
muffin cups or cake cups used for little cup cakes

METHOD

Heat oven to 400 degrees F. Grease and flour the bottoms of 12 medium cup cake (or muffin) tins (2 1/2" x 1 1/4"). Beat egg and stir in milk and oil (or margarine). Put in remaining ingredients and stir lightly just once or twice so that the flour is moistened. The batter will be lumpy. Fill the tins about three-quarters full. Bake until golden brown for about 20 minutes. Remove from tin immediately. Eaten straight off with a little butter, or jam or just plain makes a tasty and healthy breakfast.

This basic recipe can be played around with in a number of ways adding variety to a breakfast staple.

Apple-Nut Muffins. A small apple, peeled, cored and chopped fine may be added to the milk and oil. A pinch of cinnamon powder to the flour and you have a new flavour in your muffins.

Banana Muffins. Reduce the milk to just 1/3 cup and add a cup of mashed banana in its place.

Honey muffins. Substitute honey for the sugar. Also add a heaped teaspoon of orange rind to the milk and oil mixture.

Nuts may be added to any of the mixtures.

Cornflake Macaroons

INGREDIENTS

2 egg whites
pinch of salt
2/3 cup castor sugar
1 tsp vanilla essence

2 cups cornflake cereal
1 cup desiccated coconut
1/2 cups pecans or sultanas

METHOD

Beat egg whites with salt until foamy. Gradually add the sugar, continuing to beat till stiff and glossy. Beat in vanilla essence. Lightly fold in cornflakes, coconut and nuts. On a greased baking tray drop into rounded shapes using a teaspoon. Leave space between each drop because they will spread when baking. Bake at 180 degrees C until pinkish brown. Takes about 10 -12 minutes. Allow to cool before storing in airtight container. These macaroons are not too sweet but are chewy and crunchy. This recipe makes about 24-30 macaroons.

Turkish Delight

INGREDIENTS

2 tbsps unflavoured gelatine
1 cup water
2 cups castor sugar
1/4 cup almonds (unblanched), toasted and coarsely chopped
1 1/2 tsp rose water
few drops red or yellow food colouring
1/2 cup sifted icing sugar
1 tbsp cornflour

METHOD

Soften gelatine in half cup of the water. Set aside. In a saucepan combine sugar and remaining water and first heat slowly, stirring all the time to dissolve the sugar. Then allow it to boil rapidly until the mixture arrives at a gel consistency. That is, when a drop of syrup is dropped into cold water it forms a gel. Now stir in the gelatine mixture until it dissolves and then remove from heat. Put in almonds, colouring and flavouring. Pour mixture into an eight-inch square tin and allow to cool completely. Using an oiled knife cut into desired squares. Combine the icing sugar and cornflour and toss squares in this mixture till they are well coated. Place in an airtight container, sprinkling any leftover icing sugar mixture between layers. Keep cool.

Indian Butter Cookies

INGREDIENTS

2 cups flour
1/2 to 3/4 cup corn oil
1/2 cup powdered sugar
1/8 tsp baking soda

1 tbsp margarine
1/4 tsp powdered cardamoms
1 tbsp grated nuts

METHOD

Sift flour and add to it the baking soda, powdered cardamoms, sugar and mix with the margarine. Add the corn oil slowly, gently bringing the flour into crumbling consistency. Mix, do not knead. When all the oil is added you should have a dough which can be shaped comfortably into small balls. Place on baking sheet or tray, gently dent in the centre or prick with fork and put in some chopped nuts on top.

Bake in preheated oven at 350 degrees F for about 10-12 minutes.

Irish Tea Bread

INGREDIENTS

12 tbsp strong tea (without milk or sugar)
2 cups mixed fruits (raisins, sultanas, dates, walnuts, cashews, almonds)
1 3/4 cup sugar
2 eggs
1/2 cup butter
1/2 cup preserved fruits such as pumpkin, ginger or pineapple preserve.
3 cups flour
1 level tsp bicarbonate of soda

METHOD

Strain the black tea and soak the mixed fruit to which you have added the sugar, overnight.

Cream eggs and butter. Add the soda to the flour and mix well. Fold in flour in the egg-butter mixture alternating with the tea mixture. Add the chopped preserves. End with a tablespoon of flour mixture.

Pour the batter in a 12-14 inch loaf tin and bake at 350 degrees F. It will take between one and one and a half hours to bake. Check to see if done with a toothpick. After the oven is put off let the Irish bread remain in for another five minutes and then remove. Allow to cool for ten minutes before removing the bread from the baking tin. Cool and cut.

No-Bake Cheesecake (vegetarian)

INGREDIENTS

The crust:

1 cup graham-cracker crumbs
1/4 cup fine (not icing) sugar
4 Tbsps butter

The cake

package lemon Jelly or Jell-0 gelatin dessert
1 cup boiling water
2 packages soft cream cheese (* 8 oz packages)
1/2 cup sugar
1 tsp vanilla
1 cup thick cream or 1 envelope Dream Whip

METHOD

First make the crust. Melting the butter. Crush the graham crackers in a blender/chopper till crumbly. Add the sugar and butter to the crumbs and mix them in a bowl. Then press this mixture into bottom of a 9 - inch sqare or circular dish, One that will also be used to serve the cake in. A springform pan may also be used, in which the bottom will be removed before serving. Refrigerate this crust.

Dissolve lemon jello in boiling water and chill till the jello is just about quarter ways set. At this point the consistency is that of unbeaten egg whites.

Put in the cream cheese, sugar and vanilla in a large bowl and beat with an electric mixer until fluffy. Add the Jello mixture and beat together. Keep away in refrigerator while preparing the cream.

Beat cream until thick. Fold the cream into the cream-cheese mixture. Then pour it into the crust. Use a butter knife to smooth over. Cover with plastic wrap and refrigerate for several hours before serving.

Fruit and Nut Bars

INGREDIENTS

1 1/2 cup sifted white flour with 2 level tsps baking powder
1/2 cup butter or margarine
1/2 cup sugar
1/2 cup brown sugar
2 eggs
1/2 tsp nutmeg
1/4 tsp cinnamon
1 tbsp finely chopped ginger preserve
1/4 cup chopped walnuts
1 cup chopped fruits (dates, raisins)

METHOD

Set oven to heat at 350 degrees F. Cream together the butter, sugar and dry spices till light and fluffy. Blend in the brown sugar and mix in half a cup of flour. Add eggs one at a time, beating well. Add the flour slowly alternating with the fruits and nuts and the chopped ginger preserve. The mixture is usually thick but light. If it appears too dry you may add a few tablespoons of milk. Pour batter into an 8" square tin or a loaf tin. Bake in preheated oven for about 35-45 minutes. Remove from oven when done and allow to cool for ten minutes before taking it out of the baking tin. Cut into rectangular bars.

Crazy Cake (Vegetarian)

INGREDIENTS

3 cups flour
2 cups sugar
6 tbsps unsweetended cocoa
2 tsps soda
1 tsp salt

3/4 cup melted shortening
or salad oil
2 tsps vinegar
2 tsps vanilla
2 cups of cold water

METHOD

Sift flour, measure, then sift again with cocoa, sugar, soda and salt. Put these dry ingredients into an ungreased 9 x 13" baking dish. Make three depressions. Put vanilla in one depression, vinegar in another and oil in the third. Pour cold water over all and using a fork, mix all together till blended, put do not beat. Bake in a moderate oven. (350 degrees F) for 40 to 50 minutes. Remove from pan and cool.

Rich Trifle Pudding (Vegetarian)

INGREDIENTS

1 packet strawberry jelly
2 1/2 cups of milk
3/4 cup of water
3 tbsps custard powder
2 tbsps sugar
1 cup fresh cream or 2 tins of Nestle's cream

a few drops of rose essence
4 tbsps of Milo
6 tsps sugar
about 20 Marie biscuits, a cup of milk to soak them in.

METHOD

Follow directions for making jelly and keep it to set in a biggish glass or steel tray. Make custard by putting on the milk to heat till it comes to boil. In a little cup, put the custard powder, sugar and the water and make a smooth mixture. Add this to the milk when it begins to boil, lower heat and stir well to mix custard powder. When the custard is thick and tends to coat the spoon thickly, remove and keep aside. Custard needs to be kept in a warm place, otherwise it thickens further and will get lumpy.

Whip up the cream till light and fluffy. Sprinkle sugar and beat a little more. Spoon out a layer of cream on the set jelly. Then cover with all the custard. Spread it out evenly, then return to freezer immediately. After an hour remove from freezer. To the cream add the Milo and beat to blend. Spread a part of this mixture on top of the custard. Put the cup of milk to boil and soak one Marie biscuit at a time in it, removing each and arranging them on top of the Milo layer. Finish up with the last part of the Milo. Sprinkle grated chocolate to decorate. Pudding needs to be kept in the freezer for the first four hours and then brought down to the fridge.

Easy Chocolate Cake

INGREDIENTS

1 1/2 cups flour
1/2 cup yoghurt
1/2 cup butter or
    margarine
1 cup sugar
1 tsp baking powder

1/2 tsp soda bicarbonate
3 tbsps cocoa
1 tsp vanilla essence
2 eggs
1/2 cup chopped walnuts

METHOD

Sift flour, baking powder and soda together. Beat butter and sugar till light. Add eggs one at a time. Add the sifted ingredients alternately with the beaten curds. Dissolve the cocoa in two or three tablespoons of milk and add the mixture slowly. Finally add the essence. Mix well and pour in greased and floured, nine-inch cake tin. Bake for 30 minutes at 350 degrees F. When cake is done, remove from tin and allow to cool for at least four hours before icing it.

Chocolate butter icing : 150 gms butter, 300 gms icing sugar, 3 tbsp cocoa, few drops vanilla essence. Beat till light and fluffy then spread over the cake evenly. A butter knife dipped in warm water works well for giving a smooth top. Sprinkle the walnuts on top.

Quick Crisp Dessert

INGREDIENTS

4 thick slices stale white bread
50 gms butter
4 apples (sweet)
100 gms sugar

METHOD

Spread the butter on the bread, leaving about a tablespoon for later use. First place two slices flat on a buttered oven proof dish, with the buttered side up. Peel the apples and slice. Place on the bread and sprinkle with sugar. Add the second layer of buttered bread, apples and sugar. Use the butter kept aside to dot over the apples. Bake for about half an hour at 450 degrees. When the apple slices are browned, the dessert is ready. Should be eaten warm.
This is also a healthy breakfast.

Apple Upside-Down Cake

INGREDIENTS

3 large, sweet apples
2 eggs
pinch of salt
1/4 cup sugar
1/2 cup flour

1/4 cup melted butter
1 tbsp lemon juice
1 1/4 cup sugar
1/4 cup water

METHOD

Using the last two ingredients listed, sugar and water prepare the caramel. Put the sugar in a pan (a heavy non-stick frying pan works well) and add the water. Keep pan on a low heat and allow the sugar to melt slowly, and then brown to a pale gold color, stirring continously.

Pour the caramel into an 8" cake tin and allow to coat the base and sides as much as possible. Meanwhile, peel, core and slice apples and keep aside. Sprinkle with lemon juice immediately. Mix the eggs and sugar in a bowl and beat till the mixture is soft and creamy yellow. Add the salt. Fold in flour and melted butter alternating in small quantities.

To put it all together: arrange apple slices on the cooled caramel. The first layer should be neat and well designed. This is the layer which will show when the cake is upturned for serving. Then add the rest of the apple in even layers. Pour the cake mixture over these and bake for about forty minutes at 375 degrees. Turn the cake out of the tin immediately. This cake can be eaten hot or cold. It is a good brunch addition.

Fresh Apple Cake

INGREDIENTS

4 cups of peeled and
   chopped apples
2 cups of sugar
1 cup of chopped walnuts
1/2 cup oil
2 eggs

2 tsps vanilla
2 cups flour
2 tsps soda
2 tsps cinnamon
1/2 tsp salt

METHOD

In a large bowl mix together the apples, sugar and walnuts. Add the oil, lightly beaten eggs and vanilla. Add the soda, cinnamon and salt to the flour then add this in big spoonfuls to the apple mixture. The batter does not need vigorous beating but just enough mixing to blend the ingredients. Pour into a 9x13 lightly greased glass dish and bake for about 40 minutes at 350 degrees.

Candy Bar Pie

INGREDIENTS

1 1/3 cup grated coconut (moist, not desiccated)
2 tbs melted butter
1 tsp instant coffee powder
2 tbs water
7 1/2 oz. bar chocolate candy bar with almonds
4 cups Cool Whip.

METHOD

Combine the coconut and butter and press into a 8" pie pan. Bake blind at 325 degrees for ten minutes. Allow to cool. Dissolve the coffee in water, then put in the chocolate which should be broken into pieces and melt over low heat. Cool. Thaw Cool Whip topping and fold into chocolate. Fill crust and then chill in freezer till firm. To slice, dip knife into water before cutting. Serve frozen.

Pineapple and Jelly Delight

INGREDIENTS

1 small can sliced pineapple	2 tbsps custard powder
	a few drops vanilla essence
1 packet (2 cup) strawberry jelly	3/4 cup fresh cream
	1 1/2 tbsps powdered sugar
1 1/2 cups milk	10 Marie biscuits, crushed
2 tsps sugar	

METHOD

Strain the pineapple and keep the syrup. Dissolve jelly in 2 cups boiling water. Add the pineapple syrup (about a cup). Using a flattish serving dish, pour half the jelly into this container and allow to set in the refrigerator.

Make custard by mixing the custard powder in half a cup of milk. Bring the rest of the milk to the boil, add sugar, reduce heat and put in the custard mixture. Stir gently, boil and remove after a minute. Let it cool.

Meanwhile beat the cream with the powdered sugar, add the vanilla essence and add the cooled custard. Blend into a smooth creamy mixture. Pour this over the set jelly and put it back in the fridge to set again. When set, sprinkle the crushed Marie biscuits on the custard and pour the second half of the jelly. Put in back in the fridge again to set. Decorate with pineapple slices and serve. Tastes as good as it looks.

Baked Semolina Pudding with Ginger and Cinnamon Sauce

INGREDIENTS

3 cups milk
1/2 cup semolina
1 egg
3 tbsps sugar
1 tbsp butter

For the sauce
1/4 tsps cinnamon powder
2 tsps ginger preserve or finely strained ginger juice
add both these ingredients to half a cup of golden syrup

METHOD

Heat milk in a pan and just before it begins to boil sprinkle the semolina and allow it to cook while you stir continuosly. Reduce heat after about three minutes and add sugar and the beaten egg. Mix well and pour into a baking dish, dot with butter and bake in a moderate oven for twenty minutes. Meanwhile make the sauce by mixing all the ingredients together and heating it. When the pudding is ready pour the sauce over it and put back to bake for ten more minutes. You may sprinkle some walnuts or cashewnuts to decorate the pudding before serving it. It is eaten cold.

Apple-Ginger Tarts

INGREDIENTS

250 gms thick apple puree
15 gms crystallised ginger
4 tbsps whipped cream

250 gms short crust dough
(recipe below)
1 tbsp apricot jam

For garnishing

icing sugar
12 glace cherries
small pieces of crystallised ginger

METHOD

Puree the apple by peeling, coring and chopping them, then put them in a saucepan with four tablespoons of water. Cover and cook till apples are soft enough to be blended into a puree. When the puree is cooled add the ginger and beat in the whipped cream.

Line 12 small tart tins with the short crust dough and bake them slowly near the top of a preheated 300 degrees F oven for 20-25 minutes. Tart cases should be crisp and golden brown in colour. Cool. Remove tart shells from the tin and fill each one first with a little apricot jam, then with the apple-ginger filling. Dust the tops with some icing sugar. Decorate each with a cherry and piece of crystallised ginger.

Creamy Lemon Pie

INGREDIENTS

1 pie crust (same as in Cherry Delight)
3 egg yolks
1 can sweetened condensed milk
1/2 cup lemon juice concentrate or
1/4 cup fresh lemon juice
few drops yellow food colouring
1/2 cup fresh cream whipped or
1 packet Dream whip
lemon slices for decoration

METHOD

Prepare the pie crust as in the Cherry Delight recipe but do not break it up with a fork after baking as done in that recipe.

Preheat oven to 350 degrees F. Put the egg yolks in a medium size bowl and beat well. Stir in condensed milk slowly, beating well. Pour the lemon juice and add the food colouring. Pour this mixture into the prepared crust and bake for 8 - 10 minutes. Cool, then put it in the fridge to chill well. Top with the whipped cream. Decorate with lemon slices. This pie can be flavoured with kesar: dissolve a few threads of kesar in a tablespoon of milk. To complete the Indianisation of this pie, you could garnish with pista and almonds and green food colouring could be used.

Gingered Pears

INGREDIENTS

4 large ripe pears 1 tsp ginger juice
rind and juice of one lime 1 tbsp sugar
rind and juice of one orange

METHOD

Peel the rind thinly from the orange and lemon. In a pan put the rind, the juice of lime, orange, and ginger and sugar and keep on the fire. Allow the sugar to dissolve.

Peel, core and quarter the pears and put in another pan. Strain the sugar syrup over the pears, cover and cook on low flame till the pears are tender.

You can substitute pineapple, mangoes or peaches for pears. Cooking time will vary with each fruit. Also, the sugar added must be adjusted to suit the natural sweetness of the fruit.

Creamy Marshmallow Dessert

INGREDIENTS

1 box sour cream	1/2 cup dessicated coconut
1 envelope Dream Whip	1/2 cup walnuts, chopped
or 1 cup thick cream	2 tbsps sugar
1 can fruit cocktail	2 tsps vanilla
1 cup little white marshmallows	

METHOD.

Drain all the syrup from the fruit cocktail and keep aside. Using the directions on the dream whip envelope. Beat the cream. If you are using fresh cream, beat till stiff and fluffy. Cover and keep in refrigerator till you prepare the sour cream mixture. Empty sour cream in a deep bowl, one which will also be used to serve this dessert, and beat with an electric beater. Slowly add the sugar and four tablespoons of syrup from the fruit cocktail. Put the whipped cream in and beat together. Using a spatula gently fold in marshmallows, fruit cocktail, desicated coconut and walnuts. Keep aside a few nuts for decoration. Finally add the vanilla essence, fold, decorate with nuts. Cover and keep in refrigerator overnight for best results.

Fruit and Nut Dessert

INGREDIENTS

250 gms cake crumbs
4 tbsps brown sugar
1/4 tsp cinnamon powder
1 tsp chopped preserved
    ginger (optional)
4 tbsps butter

4 tbsps raisins
grated rind of half a lemon
1 tbsp lemon juice
1 large apple peeled and cut
    into little pieces

METHOD

Crumble cake in a mixing bowl and add brown sugar, cinnamon and ginger preserve to it. Put in the butter by cutting into small pieces. Mix all the other ingredients, including the juice. This mixture does not blend but remains crumbly. Turn into greased dish and bake for 20 minutes at 350 degrees F. Delicious when poured over ice-cream or as a breakfast treat. Children love it.

English Trifle

INGREDIENTS

1 large or two small packets of jelly
leftover sponge cake broken into pieces, enough to cover bottom of dish or bowl
3 tbsps sherry or any sweet red wine

1 can fruit cocktail
2 cups of custard made with custard powder according to directions on box
grated chocolate and nuts for decoration

METHOD

Dissolve the jelly as per package directions. In a glass serving dish line the bottom, with pieces of sponge cake. Spoon the sherry or wine over it, covering as much of the cake as you can. Drain the can of fruit cocktail. Some of the pieces of the fruit are often large and it is preferable to cut them smaller. Spread this fruit over the cake. Now pour the jelly mixture over fruit and sponge. Refrigerate and allow to set. When the jelly is well set make the custard. Let it cool for about fifteen minutes before you pour it over the jelly. Put it back in the fridge till serving time. Garnish with grated chocolate and nuts before you serve.

Mango Mousse

INGREDIENTS

4 ripe mangoes
1 tbsp gelatine
1/4 cup cold water
1 tbsp lemon juice

3/4 cup sugar
1 cup fresh cream whipped up to about 2 21/2 cups whipped cream

METHOD

Peel mangoes, cut and mash to a puree. Soften the gelatine in the cold water and then dissolve it over hot water. Add this smoothened mixture to the mango puree. Now add the lemon juice and sugar. Carefully fold in cream. Pour into serving dish or individual bowls and refrigerate.

Cherry Delight

INGREDIENTS

For the crust
2 cups flour
1/2 cup brown sugar
1 cup finely chopped nuts
   (cashew or walnuts or
   almonds)

Filling
200 gms packet cream
   cheese
1 cup powdered sugar
1 tsp vanilla
1 cup fresh cream whipped or
2 envelopes Dream Whip
2 cans or 4 cups Cherry Pie
   Filling

METHOD

To make the crust: Mix crust ingredients and press into 9" ×13" pan and bake this for 15 minutes at 400 degrees F. Using a fork crumble the crust into pieces and leave in the pan.

For the filling: Mix the softened cream cheese with powdered sugar, add vanilla. Whip up the cream till fluffy and stiff, fold in the cream cheese mixture into this. Spread this over the crumbled crust. Now top this with the cherry pie filling and refrigerate for 12 hours. Cut into squares for serving.

Apple Torte

Ingredients

For the crust :
1/2 cup butter
1/3 cup sugar
1/4 tsp vanilla
1 cup flour

For the filling :

1/4 cup sugar
200 gms cream cheese
1/2 tsp vanilla
1 tbsp custard powder or 1 egg
4 cups sliced apple
1/3 cup sugar
1/2 tsp cinnamon

Method.

Cream together the butter, sugar and vanilla for the crust, then blend in the flour. Spread on bottom and sides of a 9" spring form pan.

To make the filling : combine the cream cheese and sugar, add the custard powder and the lemon juice and vanilla and blend well. Put into pastry lined pan. Now slowly layer the top with the four cups of sliced apple. Mix together the sugar and cinnamon and sprinkle this over the apple topping.

Preheat oven to 400 degrees and bake in it for the first 10 minutes, then reduce temperature to 375 degrees and bake for 25 minutes more. Cool, chill and serve.

Short Crust Dough

INGREDIENTS

250 gms flour   125 gms butter
200 gms icing sugar   2 eggs
pinch of salt

METHOD

Sift the flour, sugar and salt together in a bowl. Add the butter and rub it in lightly with fingertips. Mixture should resemble fine breadcrumbs. Add eggs, stir with a fork. When the mixture is all moistened and begins to cling together use your hands to gently press it into a ball. Now place on floured surface and knead slowly into a smooth mass. Wrap dough in plastic wrap and refrigerate for about thirty minutes before rolling out.

Alphabetic List of Recipes

Apple Ginger Tarts
Apple Torte
Apple Upside-Down Cake
Baked Macaroni and Ham
Baked Semolina Pudding
Baked Vegetable Casserole
Basic Muffins
Black Pepper Chicken
Brinjal Curry
Cabbage Cutlets
Cabbage Manchurian
Candy Bar Pie
Capsicum Pulao
Carrot Cake
Cauliflower Spinach Sukha
Cheesy Chicken Submarine
Cheese Cake (Vegetarian)
Cheese Kofta Curry
Cherry Delight
Chicken Palak
Chicken Chilli
Chicken Chat
Chicken Royale
Chicken Satay
Chicken Curry with Cummin
Chinese Prawn Balls
Cornflake Macaroons
Crazy Cake (vegetarian)

Creamy Lemon Pie
Creamy Marshmallow Dessert
Easy Chocolate Cake
Egg Cutlests
Egg Vindaloo
English Trifle
Fettuchini Alfredo
Fresh Apple Cake
Fried Chicken leg
Fried Prawn Rice
Fruit and Nut Dessert
Fruit and Nut Bars
Fruity Cabbage Salad
Ginger Flavoured Cauliflower
Gingered Pears
Goanese Potato
Greek Macaroni Salad
Ground Mutton Pie
Green Peas and Cashew Nut Curry
Hyderabad Chicken
Indian Butter Cookies
Indonesian Curry
Instant Lasagna
Irish Tea Bread
Lunch Box Puris
Macaroni Mushroom Bake
Malai Kofta with an Italian Touch
Mango Mousse
Mushrooms Au Gratin
Mushroom with Yoghurt
Mutton Pasanda
Mutton Curry
Mutton Chops with Yoghurt
Mutton Vindaloo
Nutritious Oatmeal biscuits
Paneer Cashew Nut Curry
Party Fried Chicken
Party Prawn Curry
Party Vegetarian Lasagna
Peas Mushroom Curry

Pineapple and Jelly Delight
Pork Ribs in Sweet and Sour Sauce
Potato and Eggplant Curry
Potato Scones
Potatoes in Green Gravy
Quick Cook Dal-Cha
Quick Fish Tikas
Quick Crisp Dessert
Rich Indian Chicken Curry
Rich Mutton Mutanjan
Rich Trifle Pudding
Russian Tea Cakes
Sauteed Mushrooms
Savoury Gram Flour Cake
Seyal Cheese Macaroni Bake
Short Crust Dough
Singapore Noodles
Spicy Chicken Wings
Spicy Mixed Vegetable Pie
Spinach Mushroom Bake
Sri Lankan Fish Curry
Sukha Eggpiant
Sukha Okra
Tuna Roll-ups
Turkish Delight

STERLING BOOKS ON COOKERY

INDIAN COOK BOOK
N. Kaushi Bhatia, 1991, ...0542 4, 174pp, Rs.50

PUNJABI COOKING
T. Premjit Gill, 1993, ...0179 8, 134pp, Rs.60

CHINESE COOKERY: VEGETARIAN DELICACIES
Sangeeta Khanna, 1992, ...0938 1, 120pp, Rs.90

PARTY CUISINE
Sangeeta Khanna, 1994, ...1534 9, 120pp, Rs.55

A COOK'S TOUR OF SOUTH INDIA
Vimla Patil, 1992, ...0947 0, 144pp, Rs.50

INDIAN COOKERY
Pritam Uberoi, 1993, ...0018 x, 158pp, Rs.50

DELIGHTS OF INDIAN APPETIZERS: PICKLES, MURABBAS, CHUTNEYS, JELLIES, SAUCES, SQUASHES, JUICES, JAMS, MARMALADES
Pritam Oberoi & Nimmi Oberoi, 1993, ...1353 2, 80pp, Rs.45

PURE VEGETARIAN INDIAN COOKERY
Pritam & Nimmi Oberoi, 1993, ...1327 3, 142pp, Rs.50

NON-VEGETARIAN INDIAN COOKERY
Pritam & Nimmi Oberoi, 1994, ...1408 3, 148pp, Rs.60

INDIAN & MUGHLAI RICE TREATS
G. Padma Vijay, 1992, ...1070 3, 136pp, Rs.45

COOKING THE HEALTHY WAY
G. Padma Vijay, 1993, ...1354 0, 96pp, Rs.45

BARBECUE
Shabnum Gupta, 1995, ...1735 X, 112pp, Rs. 30

CHINESE CUISINE
Kasturi Rangachari, 1995, ...1733 3, 112pp, Rs. 30

DESSERTS
Kasturi Rangachari, 1995, ...1739 2, 112pp, Rs. 30

SOUPS
Kasturi Rangachari, 1995, ...1732 5, 112pp, Rs. 30

PASTA DELIGHTS
Shukla Rudra, 1995, ...1738 4, 112pp, Rs. 30

MEAT DELIGHTS
Shabnum Gupta, 1995, ...1741 4, 112pp, Rs. 30

POTATO DELIGHTS
Prem Nargas, 1995, ...1734 1, 112pp, Rs. 30

CHOCOLATE DELIGHTS
Neelaxi Arora, 1995, ...1736 8, 112pp, Rs. 30

SALADS
1994, ...1695 7, 112pp, Rs. 25

MUGHLAI CUISINE
1994, ...1692 2, 112pp, Rs. 25

CAKES
1994, ...1693 0, 112pp, Rs. 25

COCKTAILS
1994, ...1694 9, 112pp, Rs. 25

SEAFOODS
1994, ...1751 1, 48pp, Rs. 35

SOUPS
1994, ...1752 x, 48pp, Rs. 35

SALADS
1994, ...1750 3, 48pp, Rs. 35

CAKES
1994, ...1749 x, 48pp, Rs. 35